To Stu,
Thank you for your support of
our Nation's Veterans!

Purple Hearts &
Wounded Spirits

Brian D. Moore

8/2016

BRIAN D. MOORE
SFC, US ARMY, RETIRED

Foreword by Governor Mike Huckabee

D0878346

A DIVISION OF
LIBERTY UNIVERSITY
Lynchburg, VA
www.LibertyMountainPublishing.com

PRAISE FOR *PURPLE HEARTS AND WOUNDED SPIRITS*

Purple Hearts and Wounded Spirits is about what it means to be an American, a soldier, a husband, a father, a sinner and a saint when called into combat against the terror visited upon one's own country. *Purple Hearts and Wounded Spirits* is Brian Moore's story and the story of many soldiers like him, who have had to go into combat and fight an enemy that is as elusive as evil itself. Moreover, this book represents the internal battle that rages when a redeemed life must enter into dark places and confront evil. This heartfelt book is a labor of love that represents the honor, the humor, the hope and the heartache that has been the grit and greatness of American fighting men and women of faith throughout every conflict.

~ Dr. Frederick J. Williams
Pastor of Faith Baptist Church,
Founder and Licensed Therapist at
Greater Manchester Christian Counseling Services
in Manchester, New Hampshire

You can contact Brian D. Moore at bdmoore@liberty.edu

Liberty Mountain Publishing
1971 University Blvd.
Lynchburg, VA 24502
www.LibertyMountainPublishing.com

Scripture quotations taken from the *New American Standard Bible*, Copyright ©
1960, 1962, 1963, 1968, 1971, 1972, 1973, 1975, 1977, 1995
by The Lockman Foundation. Used by permission (www.Lockman.org).

First edition, October 2015

ISBN: 978-1-935986-80-5

Cover and Interior Book Design by Coreen Montagna

Printed in the United States of America

This book is dedicated to all of the American Veterans who stood up and sacrificed their health and even their lives in defense of their fellow Americans.

TABLE OF CONTENTS

Acknowledgment 1

Foreword 3

Author's Note 5

Introduction 7

Section I
Chapter 1: 9/11 19
Chapter 2: First Tour: Answering the Call 25

Section II
Chapter 3: Wheels Up 35
Chapter 4: Kuwait 37
Chapter 5: Kurdistain 41
Chapter 6: Missions to Save Gilligan 45
Chapter 7: Human Sheilds 51
Chapter 8: On the Lighter Side 55
Chapter 9: The Red Cross 59
Chapter 10: I Didn't See That Coming 61

Section III
Chapter 11: The Homecoming 65
Chapter 12: Fort Hood 69
Chapter 13: Kabul 73
Chapter 14: Yellow Dog 77
Chapter 15: My Dances with Wolves: Fort Apache 85
Chapter 16: Border Wars 97
Chapter 17: Night Raids 107
Chapter 18: Back to Yellow Dog 115
Chapter 19: Back to School 121
Chapter 20: Headed Home 125
Chapter 21: The Beginning of the End: Groundhog Day 135
Chapter 22: Purple Hearts and Wounded Spirits 149

Epilogue 155

Acronyms, Abbreviations, and Military Jargon 159

References 162

About the Author 163

ACKNOWLEDGMENT

There are so many friends and family to acknowledge for their support with the writing of this book. Yet the primary acknowledgment must go to my wife Raquel for her unconditional love throughout all of the trials and tribulations of our deployments. I must also recognize my sister Carole and brothers Ray and Paul for their steadfast support of my family during my deployments.

FOREWORD

Though my bid for the White House in 2008 fell short, one great blessing from the process was meeting remarkable people who love their country and their fellow man and who truly make America great. Brian Moore is one of those people that I had the pleasure to meet during a campaign trip to Londonderry, New Hampshire in 2008 when Senator Bob Clegg of New Hampshire introduced Brian to Chuck Norris and me.

Brian's service in the military became personal after 9/11, and during his three tours to Iraq and Afghanistan he distributed all kinds of useful and practical items like pens, toiletries, and even soccer balls to soldiers and to locals. His making such welcomed items available donated from friends and family back home caused his fellow soldiers to call his efforts "Moore Mart" and the name and the project stuck. Moore Mart has made the lives of soldiers and citizens of the war zone more tolerable and livable.

As you read Brian's story, you will discover the powerful narrative of the kind of heroism that makes America the greatest nation on earth. It's the story of a man, his faith, his resilience, and his commitment to let God use him to help others. It's the story of an unselfish man seeking to serve and being found faithful. Brian Moore is my kind of hero!

~Governor Mike Huckabee

AUTHOR'S NOTE

It is not my intention to delve into deep theological debate, I am merely attempting to relate what I believe happened during my three tours and how that affected me then and now.

In the attempt to find some rational explanation for the 9/11 attacks and avoiding as much of the political rhetoric as possible, I share with you only what I believe to be true. The following is one man's, one soldier's, one Christian's account of September 11, 2001, and his subsequent journey.

INTRODUCTION

September 11, 2001, changed everything in my life. I, like thousands of others, was angry and appalled by what our enemies had done, especially to so many innocent people. This was also a very personal attack as my oldest son, Brandon (a senior in a Christian high school) and his classmates were engaged in street evangelism in the lobby of the Twin Towers on September 7-10, 2001. His entire class to include advisors and teachers were distributing pamphlets and sharing the Gospel in both lobbies. The people they encountered were so receptive that they discussed staying through Monday September 11th, but decided instead to return to New Hampshire. When the news broke that both towers had been destroyed, I realized how close we had come to a family tragedy.

In the coming days I found myself possessed by anger and hatred. Not only by the acts of violence toward my country but those acts of violence were indiscriminately directed toward the innocent, like my son and his classmates. They had done nothing to these terrorists but yet, as Osama bin Laden stated, he was justified before Allah if he killed as many as three million Americans, to include women and children. The more I contemplated the horror, the more vengeful my thoughts became. I was conflicted with such foreign emotions and as a father I felt terribly burdened to protect my family somehow. I needed to stop these people from trying to hurt my family again, which I felt was inevitable, and as an American soldier I felt a sense of duty to defend my country.

Before I can share where I went after 9/11, I need to start at the beginning. My family history is one of sacrifice and service, to each other, our neighbors and ultimately our country. My brothers and I were fourth-generation military. My grandfathers, father and oldest brother Ray were all noble seamen. It was my brother Paul who broke the mold and became a ground pounder in the U.S. Army, and I was not far behind him.

STAFF SERGEANT MOORE AND BROTHER RAY MOORE SAYING FAREWELL.

My father was a career, non-commissioned officer with the United States Coast Guard which meant we grew up living alongside saltwater. Our home was not a house but a ship, according to my Dad, and he tried to run it that way. My brothers and I were called by birth order. I was eight years old before I realized that my real name was not Number 3! Other than my mother I never heard anyone refer to my Dad by any title other than "Chief." A Chief Petty Officer is the equivalent to being a Sergeant in the Army.

I learned many things from my Dad, some good and some regrettable. He was not a perfect man, but he was grounded in the positive traits that I clung too; primarily, a fierce loyalty to family and country. My faith was learned from my mother. He was an alcoholic for as long as I can remember and not a friendly or happy one at that. I do not intend to speak ill of the dead, especially my own father, yet his past was my future in some ways. Later in life as I began to deal with my own demons through self-medication, I understood where my Dad may have been coming from. I can only imagine what demons he was running from. I was determined, however, not to raise my children under the same darkness that vexed my father; I wanted that cycle broken.

We are a family that is not afraid to do the right thing regardless of the consequences and are no strangers to adversity because of our desire to serve and go. My brother Ray served in the United States Coast Guard (USCG), nearly losing his life on several missions to rescue distressed seafarers. My brother Paul, while serving in the United States Army in Korea, was injured in a parachuting accident that left him paralyzed. My sister Carole overcame the horror of the terrorist bombing of the federal building in Oklahoma City. She stayed home that day with a sick child and her office was destroyed. There is no doubt that had Carole gone to work that day she would have been killed by the explosion. Carole's husband Terry had a key role in dealing with the terrorist actions on 9/11 as a Federal Aviation Administration official and would later spend a year in Iraq developing their civilian aviation air traffic control network.

SERGEANT FIRST CLASS MOORE AND TERRY BIGGIO IN BAGHDAD.

My family was well grounded with a sense of service to family and country; we did not shy away from hardship. We understood that to hide from danger and from those who mean you ill only invites more of the same. To quote author and founding father Thomas Paine, "If there must be trouble, let it be in my day, that my child may have peace."

During my first tour to Iraq something very cool happened. My sister Carole asked what I needed since it was difficult to acquire basic items there. This could include snacks that were easy to take on convoys to baby wipes. She also asked if she could send stuff for my buddies. I thought that was a great idea and encouraged her to send all of us items. Well not only did she send care packages, she addressed each one to the individual soldier by name. Each package contained a variety of items that I had suggested would be helpful. The response from the guys was surprising and humorous. They were very taken by the fact that the packages were addressed to them but also the variety of items. When one of the soldiers joked that "your family has more stuff than Wal-Mart," I was from then on forever tagged with the nickname "SGT Mooremart."

Seeing how many of the soldiers appreciated getting personalized care packages, my sister Carole and brother Paul decided to start Mooremart (MM). MM was established as a non-profit organization that would support troops and the children living in war zones throughout the Middle East. Along with the bare essentials, MM also sent cleaning supplies for our living quarters and even our weapons. The early deployments were truly lacking in logistical support to say the least. Logistics is the section of the military that provides food and bullets to the frontline troops. When a mission is in its early stages the logistics support often lags behind, hence for the need for organizations such as MM. My brother Ray sent collapsible fishing poles for the green pond we lived next to, and Carole and Paul sent radio controlled boats and cars for stress relief during our sparse downtime.

It was during my tour to Afghanistan that MM really took off from supporting my immediate unit to supporting any service member regardless of branch of service or theater of operation. Some amazing examples of MM's outreach were felt in Kuwait at the reception center. Here troops arrive and wait for "a ride to the war." During that time there is no mail from home; many of these young men are away from home and in a very different environment for the first time. Paul and Carole realized this fact and boxed up Christmas stockings full of candy and gifts and shipped them to these centers in time for that holiday season. When the troops arrived they were each given their Christmas stocking provided by fellow Americans who thought of them at this stressful time. The impact on the morale of those troops and others like them cannot be measured.

While I traveled the Middle East (especially in Afghanistan) I saw how little the local children had. This was particularly true in regards to school supplies. Afghan children walked to a school which could be nothing more than sitting on the ground under a tree. Quite often it was a mud hut with open windows, no electricity, no indoor plumbing and, most importantly, no supplies.

When I discovered that Afghan school children did not have basic classroom supplies, I asked my interpreter, "How do they learn?"

He explained that after walking miles to get to school they will sit, listen and attempt to memorize the lesson. I was knocked off my feet one day when we passed a group of children who began to yell, "Pen! Pen!" I was used to hearing calls for candy or a biscuit (especially in Iraq), not pens.

This discovery led me to ask my MM family to ship school supplies to myself and any other United States soldiers who could distribute them. The fact that a child anywhere is asking for a simple pen because they want to learn moved me, not just as a teacher but as an American who is blessed with so much. My friends and family at MM certainly stepped up and began shipping donated backpacks, pens, pencils, crayons, notebooks, erasers and the list goes on.

SCHOOL CHILDREN HAPPY TO HAVE
THEIR MOOREMART BACK PACKS AND SCHOOL SUPPLIES.

As these supplies began to arrive at our base other soldiers would spend their free time filling the backpacks with the assortment of supplies provided. We loaded the packs into our trucks and took them with us into the villages. The response was truly inspiring and far reaching. Whenever we entered into a new region we would meet with the local village elders to discuss our mission and their needs. What better way to "win hearts and minds" than by providing school supplies to their children? Eventually this plan would grow to include medical care and supplies.

The actual process of getting these packs to the children was complicated at first but rewarding in so many ways. The reality was that if we gave these supplies to the elders or even the teachers the children would never see them. According to our interpreter their culture demands that these adults provide for their own families first. Yet if we were to physically hand these packs to each child we would be certain they had received them and could keep them. In the Afghan culture if someone gives you a gift no one will take it away from you.

Realizing that the girls in Afghanistan were last on every list we insisted that the soldiers give school supplies to the girls first and then to the boys. Some locals were not happy with that idea since they most likely were not educating their own daughters. I advised them that if the girls did not receive packs then no one would get them, so they submitted to our standard. That was also MM's standard for any program that they supported in either Iraq or Afghanistan.

Words cannot describe the feeling I got when I would see children walking to school with backpacks filled with school supplies. I realized that with MM's help we had changed the lives of generations of Afghans. I say that knowing that when a child learns to read the entire world opens up to them. This is especially true in countries like Afghanistan where girls are poorly educated. Once grown, a literate mother can teach her children to read and write, potentially lifting an entire generation out of poverty.

To better support these types of needs for troops and local families, MM needed to seek the support of friends both locally and across the nation. One such event was a drive to raise support for sporting equipment, especially soccer balls.

Soccer is a very popular sport around the world and providing our troops with soccer balls to hand out to local children and schools is a great way to open doors for friendship. In the eight years that Mooremart ran the soccer ball program, Mooremart volunteers were able to ship over forty-seven hundred soccer balls to the Middle East that were then distributed to local children living throughout Iraq and Afghanistan.

On January 5, 2008, Governor Mike Huckabee and Chuck Norris spoke at a "Reason for Giving" at Londonderry Middle School cafeteria in Londonderry, NH. At the event Governor Huckabee and Chuck Norris donated a number of soccer balls to Mooremart's soccer ball program. Mooremart presented the governor and Norris with a Mooremart T-shirt and thanked them for their service to our country and their support of our military. The support of great Americans like Governor Huckabee and Chuck Norris cannot be overstated, as their help brought the attention and support that MM needs to continue its mission.

Chuck Norris stayed late after the event and signed twenty-five flags and T-shirts that were sent to my unit in Iraq as well as others throughout the Middle East. Soon from across the Middle East United States soldiers were asking for a Chuck Norris Mooremart T-shirt or a Chuck Norris flag for their Humvees.

MY BROTHER PAUL MOORE WITH CHUCK NORRIS
AT A 2008 MOOREMART SOCCER BALL DRIVE.

MY SISTER CAROLE AND BROTHER PAUL
AT MOOREMART'S 50,000th CARE PACKAGE EVENT.

A SECTION OF MY PLATOON DISPLAYS A FLAG THAT SOME SCHOOL CHILDREN
HAD MADE LITERALLY BY HAND, COURTESY OF MOOREMART.

SANTA'S HAPPY ELF SGT BOUDREAU HELPING SFC MOORE DISTRIBUTE
CHRISTMAS STOCKINGS SUPPLIED BY MOOREMART TO THE TROOPS IN BAGHDAD.

It is events like this that allowed the folks at MM to step up and provide so many with so much. Through the last ten years MM developed into a community based group that sends care packages to each specific soldier in their name with the specific items that they had requested. Since September of 2014, MM has shipped more than sixty-five thousand individual care packages! During the August 2014 packing event, MM celebrated over ten years of service.

AMERICAN AND AFGHAN SOLDIERS
DISTRIBUTING SCHOOL SUPPLIES, PROVIDED BY MOOREMART.

SECTION I

CHAPTER ONE

9/11

I would imagine that life before 9/11 was similar to that prior to the Attack on Pearl Harbor on December 7, 1941, or even before the assassination of President John F. Kennedy (JFK). Americans of every race, gender, ethnicity and walk of life were going through each day like nothing would change anytime soon. Fulfilling their obligations of faith, family and work as one day inevitably rolled into the next.

It was at such a time that a sudden wave of shock and disbelief rolled over our nation. An event so personally tragic that it took your breath away, yet at the same time was felt by the entire nation creating a common bond of pain, anger and even fear. Similar to the attack on Pearl Harbor, our nation was united with that sense of kinship that only comes from shared tragedy.

As much as Pearl Harbor was a premeditated act of betrayal by another nation, the Kennedy assassination was a heinous criminal act, perpetrated by a twisted individual who sought to impose his political agenda on the United States. The heart wrenching emotions of loss and betrayal were eventually followed by righteous indignation and outright anger after these events. The terrorist attack of 9/11 caused the horrific combination of emotions that were felt after Pearl Harbor and the assassination of JFK. The effort to make any sense of that event and to deal with its immediate ramifications, while striving to maintain any real sense of normalcy for my family, would become the ultimate goal of my journey.

On the morning of September 11, 2001, I was teaching history and English at a small Christian school in northern New England. I had spent the last ten years teaching and coaching in educational ministries during the day, and working as an adjunct instructor at a local college at night. My original intention for getting into the education profession was twofold: I wanted to be on the same schedule as my children, and I really enjoyed history and thought I would be good at teaching it. My plan was to teach at a public high school and do some coaching on the side. Yet God had a better plan for my family and me.

It was during graduate school that He grabbed my attention and my heart and steered me toward a full-time ministry in education. Anyone who has worked in a Christian ministry knows all too well that making a lot of money is unrealistic, so I needed to work as many side jobs as possible.

One of my part-time jobs was the Army National Guard (ANG). I was raised in a military family where both of my older brothers and my Father had been in the military. Due to my call to ministry I knew I could not go on active duty, so I decided to serve locally with the ANG. Though I held a master's degree in education (M.Ed.), pursuing a commission as an officer would not have been conducive to my work and family obligations.

Many people in the ANG, especially the officers, had difficulty understanding why, with my level of education, I would not pursue a commission as an officer as opposed to a career as a non-commissioned officer (NCO)—a soldier who holds a sergeants rank. I discovered that this was a terrific opportunity to evangelize by sharing what God had done in and through my life in regards to the ministries that I was involved with. The realization that there were circumstances in my life that were bigger than my own desires and aspirations confused some people, but it made perfect sense in my Christian worldview.

By the time I was told about the 9/11 attack, both planes had already crashed into the World Trade Center and the other two were not far behind. The staff at our school pulled all students out of class and assembled everyone in the cafeteria to watch the news together. Like most Americans, we did not have much information to go on but as soon as I saw the video of both planes hitting the towers there was no doubt in my mind that this was a coordinated attack. The important questions were: by whom and why?

Although I eventually discovered the answers to those questions, the initial reaction by most of the people around me varied little. They were trying to come to grips with the shock of what had just happened and were realizing that this was not a movie. Real people were leaping to certain death to keep from being burned alive. Once we learned that two other planes had crashed, it was painfully obvious that we were under attack.

The school staff soon realized that we were not watching the news alone and had a room full of teenagers with us. These students were looking to us for some kind of assurance that everything was going to be alright. We took them back to class and tried to process what had just happened with the best perspective we had. With no idea of where or when the next attack would take place, parents began picking their children up from school, wanting to keep them close; I imagine that scenario was repeated around the country that afternoon.

Later that evening, the attack was the obvious topic of discussion around the dinner table. For my oldest son, Brandon, who was a senior at a Christian high school, this was an especially painful and powerful event to process because he had just returned from a weekend mission trip to New York City (NYC), specifically doing street evangelism in front of the Twin Towers just two days prior.

He came home from NYC talking about how scary it was to be standing on the streets of NYC approaching total strangers asking them about their relationship with Jesus Christ. During the three days his class spent there, he estimates that they spoke to over one thousand people. Brandon was pleasantly surprised with the positive response he received from most of the people he spoke with. I commented that it was a definite sign that the Holy Spirit was standing beside him and his friends as they shared the Gospel.

My son, looking for a positive take on the 9/11 events, wondered if any of the people that he spoke with might have made a decision for Christ, either that weekend or even at the moment prior to their horrific death. We discussed how he will not know the answer to that question until he's in Heaven, but how glorious that realization would be. Until then we can only pray for peace and comfort for the families of those lost on 9/11 and remember how important evangelism is.

I was impressed with his response to a terribly painful event, yet I could not get past the feeling of being kicked in the gut. That sick feeling was born out of fear for my own family and of a growing anger toward those who did this horrible thing in the name of their god. I realized that had the planes crashed on Friday or had his class decided to stay through Monday they would likely be crushed under tons of debris from those towers. My son and his friends, all decent kids with futures that promised to make the world spin a little better, would be gone; and for what? What had they ever done to anyone else, not to mention people half-a-world away, that someone would feel truly justified in murdering them?

Over the next few months anger began to burrow deep into my heart, to the point that I was consumed with it and the fear that I could not protect my family from another attack. The more I thought about it the more vengeful I became. As a father I felt terribly burdened to defend my family somehow. I needed to stop these people from trying to hurt my family ever again.

Over the next couple years I continued teaching and eventually became an administrator at that same Christian school. My son graduated high school and went on to college while my younger children continued with life like not much had changed. My wife Raquel, however, knew that things had changed with me and for us. We watched and cheered as President George W. Bush sent bombers and troops into Afghanistan to topple the Taliban-led government and deny Al Qaeda a safe haven from which to base their terror operations.

The ANG had stepped up its combat training and prep for our possible deployment and Raquel was suddenly introduced to the reality of what an eventual deployment would mean to her and the children.

In January 2003, while I was breaking the ice off from the hayloft door of our garage, I lost my footing and fell from the second floor. I landed feet first and rolled to the ground, a challenge in and of itself since the driveway was frozen solid in the sub-zero temperature. I lay there for a moment in tremendous pain realizing that I had really screwed up this time. I did not try to stand but crawled from the garage to the front door of our house. By the time I reached the door I was beginning to pass out from the pain and hypothermia.

I managed to knock on the door and my six year old daughter Bekah answered; she looked at me on the ground, assumed I was playing a game, and said, "Oh, Daddy," and closed the door in my face. Just as I was sure I would die on my own front steps Raquel opened the door, she had asked Bekah who was at the door and Bekah said, "Daddy, he's on the ground, silly Daddy." I told Raquel what had happened and suggested she take me to the emergency room in our car; of course she knew better and called for an ambulance. Later the x-rays would show that I had broken both of my legs just above the ankle, but the doctor stated that I was lucky I did not injure my back, which is common during such falls.

I tell this story for a few reasons. First to share what a crazy life I led at times, and second, to show that my Bekah is precious and a character to say the least. More importantly this was January of 2003; I did not know that in less than one year I would be deployed to Iraq with legs that were not completely healed. I could not attend any more ANG drills that year and focused on teaching from a wheelchair and eventually crutches. I developed a new appreciation for Raquel that year; with two broken legs life gets complicated for even the simple things like getting dressed and going to the bathroom. I was forced to accept more help than I felt comfortable with, being a generally independent and stubborn person.

The year passed—as quickly as most—and before I knew it we were hanging Christmas decorations. I was walking without crutches by then, with only a removable leg cast for my right leg. Due to the location of the breaks it would be a long time before I would be able to walk far without experiencing a significant amount of pain. Sitting at the kitchen table I received a call from a sergeant (SGT) from the ANG. This was not a big deal as they called periodically to check on my progress.

I could tell by the tone of his voice that something was different; he advised me that our unit was being activated to deploy to the Middle East. "To do what?" I asked since we were an artillery unit and I knew we were not dragging our Howitzers (heavy cannons) all the way to Iraq.

"To be combat MPs," he replied.

"What's the difference between a regular MP and a combat MP?" I asked.

"We get to shoot back," he said in grave seriousness.

The SGT advised me that they realized that I was in no condition to deploy but that I needed to respond to the "call up" until I was medically excused from active service.

"If I did deploy with the unit, how long would we be gone?" I asked him.

"Approximately eighteen months," he replied.

"Eighteen months!" I said.

I thanked him and told him that I would be at the armory as advised. I hung up the phone and turned to see Raquel standing there fighting back the tears.

"Eighteen months! That's a year and half without you here!" she said.

During our eleven years of marriage we had not been separated for more than a few days; the thought of being a world away for more than a year was daunting to say the least.

"But they said I don't have to go," I told her, trying to ease her fears.

"Who are you kidding? Nothing could keep you here," she said as she turned and walked into the bedroom closing the door behind her.

I sat alone in the kitchen feeling completely lost. What should I do? What could I do? There were so many contradicting forces pulling at me, not to mention the internal voices motivated by my anger over 9/11. I held a deep sense of patriotism as well as an obligation to honor my oath to answer the call of my country. Yet I had a legitimate medical reason to not go. I could still help by staying back and supporting the effort from home. I was torn.

I realized that I had been considering how the attack on 9/11 had impacted me, hoping to get the chance to take the fight to the enemy and in some small way defend my family.

Yet after seeing the look in my wife's eyes, I was suddenly brought back to the world of here and now where my wife would be home alone and look after everything herself. She would be paying the bills, taking care of four children and selling our house that was still on the market. I realized that while many families went through deployments—my own mother was often alone when my dad was out to sea—it's different when it's your wife and your children. The guilt was overwhelming and well deserved; I knew what I had to do.

CHAPTER TWO

FIRST TOUR: ANSWERING THE CALL

I reported in at the Armory on a very cold and snowy December morning. My ANG command had already stated that they did not expect me to deploy with them due to the fact that I had broken both of my legs in an accident at home less than a year prior. Yet I was nervous, not knowing what to expect from a process with which I had no prior experience. I was anxious about my impending decision as to whether I would volunteer to deploy or not.

It had already been a long day by the time we "formed up" for roll call. I had transferred to this Armory just prior to my accident. I accepted a promotion to Staff Sergeant (SSG) but in doing so I had to change Armories, which meant a three hour drive one way, one weekend per month. I barely knew any of the other soldiers because of this, which added to my anxiety. I found myself wishing I had remained with my former unit, thinking that at least if I deployed I would be going with guys I had known and trained with for years. Hindsight is usually clearer and looking back I am certain that I was exactly where the Lord wanted me to be.

During first formation, we were given a basic rundown of the mobilization process, both short and long term. The other soldiers were assigned to their respective squads and positions and I was told to report to the First Sergeant. It was at that point that I knew that I needed to deploy. I had enlisted with every intention of "answering the call" of my country if it came to that. I believed that I needed to go with the soldiers of my unit, to stand with them regardless of my physical pain or the outcome of our deployment. Even though I was still dealing with the emotions of anger and revenge brought on by the 9/11 attacks, at that moment my mind was clear and my decision was right.

The First Sergeant began to explain what my position and duties would be while the unit was deployed. I stopped him and stated that after much prayer and consideration I wanted to volunteer to go with our unit to Iraq. He hesitated for a moment and then with a curious smile asked me if I was physically up to the possible demands of combat in Iraq. The word "combat" stunned me. Until then all I heard were terms like "deployment" or "tour of duty." The realization of what that term meant hit me square in the chest. The same enemy that had murdered our friends here would be in Iraq in great numbers and well-armed.

"Absolutely," I replied. "I'm ready and I cannot imagine watching my brothers leave for war while I stayed behind."

The First Sergeant was pleased with my answer and stated that he would move to have my orders amended. He appreciated my sense of duty, especially considering the line that had formed outside of his office with soldiers who had a hundred reasons why they could not deploy. Some had legitimate reasons, such as a critically ill spouse, while others were far less noble. Our younger soldiers who had joined strictly for the college benefits were suddenly forced to face the reality that a contract has two sides and they were being held accountable for that. The worst case I heard of was a soldier in my unit who went home and actually beat his wife up knowing that he would be arrested and by law not be allowed to deploy. But the vast majority of soldiers that I served with left their families, jobs and college to honor their oath to defend their country.

MOBILIZATION: FORT DIX

After a month of standing in long lines at our state headquarters (HQ), filling out a mountain of paperwork in triplicate, we left for

Ft. Dix, NJ. Only the Army would send troops to New Jersey in January to prepare them for combat in the Middle East! The good-byes to my family were heart wrenching; especially hard was the look on Raquel's face as the bus pulled away. She was making every effort to keep it together and appear brave, not wanting to upset me, yet I could sense that she felt very alone for the first time in our marriage. I felt a crushing weight on my heart and for a moment I just wanted to go home.

An old Vietnam veteran shared with me the best piece of advice on dealing with this feeling. A "distracted soldier was a dead soldier," he said, suggesting that I needed to compartmentalize my life so that I was a husband and dad only when I was actually communicating with my family.

"The moment you say good-bye you are nothing less than SSG Moore. All that matters is the mission at hand and your brothers beside you. Remember that and you will return to your family again one day, God willing! Lose that focus and your family will most certainly see you again, draped with a flag!" I accepted the harsh reality of this new, necessary mind set.

Upon our arrival to Ft. Dix I was promptly promoted to SSG but since I had been late in joining the deployment I was tasked with a Team Leaders (TL) position instead of a Squad Leader (SL). Mobilization at Ft. Dix was an unnecessarily miserable experience due to a lack of preparation and incompetence on the part of the Permanent Party (PP)—the soldiers who are based at a particular installation—who were in this case tasked with getting all arriving units prepared for Mobilization to a Middle East combat zone. Our own command was weak in certain areas due to the fact that we were all thrown into this mobilization site in less than a month's time.

We were housed in old brick barracks that reeked from a combination of a defective sanitation system and mold. Having spent several years in the infantry, I was no stranger to living in uncomfortable surroundings but became aggravated when there was no excuse for it. Most of the NCOs were bunked twelve to a room and shared a common bathroom with fifty other men. Our days were extremely long, monotonous and generally pointless. We were told that we had to "check all the boxes" before we deployed to be sure we were ready. Initially, I found this insulting. We had all passed boot camp and other advanced training along with years of actual experience, yet they treated us like we had just fallen off the bus at basic training. Realistically, all we required was a maximum of two to three weeks of preparation. We needed our paperwork completed, new issue of uniforms and gear, and weapons training. As we discovered, once you arrive in the country the unit you are replacing gives you all the information you will actually need such as where you live, where you work and how to kill the enemy—all of which we learned in less than a week.

This basic level of training was amplified by the freezing temperatures that we endured for twelve hours per day outside. The infantry has a saying in regards to weather, "if it's not raining we aren't training, if it's not snowing we aren't going." Yet it is Army Standard Operating Procedure (SOP) that when troops are training in cold temperatures that a "warming tent" be provided. I mention this not to whine but as an example of the level of frustration that we endured before ever leaving this country. A warming tent is just what it sounds like. Between training events soldiers can wait inside a tent that will shelter them from the rain, snow, and wind as well as provide some heat. During the weeks that we trained at Ft. Dix in January and February, only one tent was ever provided to us and it had no stove for heat.

Training usually consisted of standing in line outside in the snow or freezing rain for hours, which eventually led to many of us becoming ill with a variety of cold weather ailments. To avoid having to deal with the reality of their poor planning and incompetence, the Base Command decided to reprimand any company leadership if one of their soldiers went to sick call for a cold weather injury, claiming that they were at fault and not the base command. This meant that no one went to sick call and we just got "unofficially" sicker. This impacted me directly when I developed the early stages of frostbite on my hands. Only Army training could give me frostbite while training for combat in the desert. My fingers swelled to the point that they were bleeding and I could no longer button my own uniform shirt and needed help getting dressed and undressed each day.

Yet during this time I became "one of the guys" with this new unit. Most of them were friendly and treated me like I had always been there. Over time I discovered that the resentment was a combination of a belief that I had taken a position from one of them and the fact (for some) that they knew I was a Christian. For most soldiers my faith was not an issue at all, while some would seek me out to discuss their fears of the impending combat, some sort counsel on the probability of dying and what that meant, while a few only saw my faith as another reason to be irritated with me.

I have never been a "Bible thumper," as that aggressiveness usually turns people away from any evangelical opportunities. I have found that those who are antagonistic toward people of faith have usually had a combination of negative past experiences and personal conviction. I certainly have not lived a perfect life, but during this deployment I knew I was representing the Christian faith to my fellow soldiers. I was much more aware of my actions and how they could either hurt or enhance my ability to share the Gospel. Paraphrasing a common theme, a Christian is just one hungry man telling another hungry man where to find bread, which is how I try to approach evangelism.

I was always aware of my testimony and that made dealing with all of the frustrations of the mobilization site even more challenging. If I moaned and groaned like some of the others, I would not be a good example of the contentment one can find through Christ. Others should be able to see a difference in Christians, one that is positive, peace filled and attractive. They should walk away asking themselves, "Why do they deal with hard times differently than I do?" It was never about what others thought of me (I could have cared less), but rather what they thought of Jesus. This became my reality and motivation as we moved toward our eventual deployment.

My first opportunity to make a difference came when I was assigned the leadership role for the following day's movement to the range (any training site that involved firing some sort of weapon system). The weather called for subzero temperatures with the windchill. This meant another day of getting to the range before sunrise, standing around freezing while waiting for the range staff to show up, and then standing in line so we could lie down in the cold, wet snow to simulate firing our weapons in the desert!

Normally, we were issued an MRE (Meal Ready to Eat or as we liked to say Meals Refused by Ethiopia) to eat during the twelve hour day we would spend on the range. I inquired of our leadership why we did not get hot soup or coffee brought out to us. I was told that we did not need anything more than MREs and that it would "toughen us up!" This statement was made by someone who almost never spent any time with the troops outside and never lost a full night's sleep or missed a hot meal. These misunderstandings and examples of failed leadership made a strong impact on how I would lead later deployments. I had learned early that when a soldier is deployed it is the little things that make a big difference, and being "tough" does not mean being miserable when it is not necessary.

I took the initiative to ask the DFAC (dining facility) staff if it was possible to get some hot food out to the range; they offered to prepare it as long as I could get someone to transport it to us. I spoke to the NCO in charge of supply and he agreed to deliver it. I also knew that the buses that transported us to and from the range were invariably late, which meant freezing soldiers standing around in the dark (after being on their feet for twelve hours). I contacted transportation and advised them that our pickup time was earlier than planned. That next day we did freeze standing around at the range, but we also had hot soup and coffee and the buses were "on time." This made a big impression on the troops and I never forgot how much it improved their morale during an otherwise miserable experience.

Unfortunately, the old adage "no good deed goes unpunished" held true and my "initiative" to make things better for the troops was not well received by some in the Chain of Command (CoC). I was verbally reprimanded for not following the preset training schedule, for accessing support from the DFAC and logistics, and most importantly, allowing the troops to realize that what I had done had always been possible. Now the troops would expect this to continue which of course meant more work on the CoC's part.

Military tradition dictates that when you are being reprimanded you do not argue your point; you just respond with "yes or no, SGT/ Sir" and accept responsibility, which I did. However when I was asked if I fully understood my role as an NCO, I replied that I did and that if placed in a similar position again I would repeat my actions. I stated that my role as an NCO was to take care of the troops while accomplishing the mission and if that meant thinking outside the box then I was willing to take responsibility for my actions. Needless to say that did not go over well and I was not given any similar leadership roles while at mobilization other than those no one else wanted to do.

One of the extra duties I was assigned was to attend the "NCO Call" at the NCO Club on base. This was an informational meeting called by the First SGT of the PP training battalion where he would put out pertinent information, reference changes in the training schedule, and to discuss any issues that the mobilization units might have. Unfortunately, it was more of a formality to demonstrate that the PP command was being proactive in regards to dealing with training issues (i.e., no warming tents at the range). However it became apparent that nothing was actually going to get addressed so these mandatory meetings were just more time wasted out of an already long day.

The test to my testimony, which also led to later internal struggles for me, was the fact that these meetings were held at the NCO Club (a bar for NCOs). Although I did not have any issues with drinking in moderation, I had not had a drink in over a decade due to my position in various Christian church and school ministries. I believed that if I accepted a position with a ministry that specifically forbade its members from drinking alcohol then I was morally obligated to abstain.

Therefore, while sitting at a table in a bar where others are drinking I "rationalized" that I was no longer directly a member of a ministry therefore I could have a drink and not be morally compromised. Notice that I said "rationalized." I had not resigned my position from the Christian school I was working at, I had just been deployed and my position would be waiting for me when I returned home. Even more important was the fact that the other soldiers saw me as a Christian and seeing me drink might create a stumbling block for them. Yet, in all honesty, I believe I drank because out of all the units at the mobilization site our unit was the only one forbidden to drink alcohol by our own CoC. This fueled my belief that if I was being ordered to attend a meeting of little importance, then I was going to have a drink to "take the edge off." This is not to say that I got hammered or drunk; I was not stupid, just prideful and stubborn.

Eventually our time at the mobilization site came to a close and we prepared for our flight to the Middle East. I was able to see Raquel, my mother, my sister Carole and her husband Terry before our unit left. I thoroughly enjoyed our time together, and I could not have been happier than when I was able to see them again, especially Raquel. I learned years later as Raquel and I began to discuss these events that she would not have come to see me again if she had realized just how painful saying good-bye again would be for her. She said, "It was like having my heart ripped out all over again since the day you loaded the bus in New Hampshire." As time went on I would learn that there were several other situations that Raquel had suffered through in silence, not wanting to burden me with concerns for her and the kids.

I believe in an adage that "if you are quick to criticize then you should be twice as quick to praise." I have already stated a few criticisms of those in various leadership roles, therefore I want to recognize and praise those in leadership that made a positive difference for us all. I specifically recall two young officers who were excellent examples of military leadership. They were outside before we were and as long as we needed to be. They ate chow last, went to bed after the troops and were always the last soldiers on every late bus regardless of time or weather conditions. I learned how to be good leader from men such as these, and it was this type of leadership that ultimately will make the worst conditions bearable and most missions successful.

SECTION II

CHAPTER THREE

WHEELS UP

Raquel and I had said our last good-byes at the mobilization site, both of us trying to appear brave and unmoved by the reality of what was happening. Before she and my mom finished their five hour drive home my unit was airborne and bound for Kuwait. During our time at the mobilization site the guys and I took notice of the huge jets that were taking off on a regular basis from the airfield just across the fence from our barracks. We frequently lamented our situation and wished that we were already on one of those flights. Most of the guys just wanted to get this thing started; the monotony and obvious uselessness of mobilization was getting to everyone.

Finally that day came; we were lined up on the tarmac, most of our gear already loaded or in route via a big metal container called a conex. I recall walking toward the stairs to load the jet, suddenly feeling sick to my stomach. I realized at that moment that this was the point of no return. For now I was still in the United States and only a few hours from home, but once that jet took off I would be a world away with no way of getting back for over a year. Separated from my wife and kids as never before, all of these thoughts were racing through my head and I began feeling nauseous. Looking back,

I wonder if I had an unrealistic belief that in order to protect my family I had to be with them all the time. This separation has taught me that ultimately they are God's children first and that His love for them is far greater than anything I could feel or do.

It was then that I noticed the soldier next to me appeared to be experiencing what I was feeling, he was pale and looked like he was about to pass out. I put my hand on his shoulder and stated that we would get through this together and that I had his back. That had a positive impact on him as he was able to board the jet. I learned an extremely important fact at that moment. If I was focused on myself I would get tunnel vision and become overwhelmed with my own fears, making me ineffective for the mission and, even worse, a liability to the other soldiers with whom I served. The understanding of that reality not only served me well throughout my three tours, it also became a part of my training for new troops being deployed on later tours.

Simply stated, your brother can cover your back better than you can as long as you are focused on looking out for each other. Everyone on the team will face certain death to save another soldier, but looking out for only you will most likely lead to paralysis by fear. I saw this played out firsthand in Baghdad during a convoy escort mission. A convoy ahead of ours had been hit which caused a ripple effect throughout the city. We halted our convoy, not able to move forward or reverse. We dismounted and watched the roof tops waiting for the inevitable attack. ; During the attack I was informed that there was a soldier under the truck behind ours. I found the soldier curled up into the fetal position crying and in a state of panic. When talking failed I grabbed the soldier by the legs, pulled her out from under the truck, disarmed her and threw her into the back of their truck, doing this while bullets and rockets were being fired at us. That event never left me; here was a soldier that was not only incapable of defending herself, but became a danger to the other soldiers with her.

CHAPTER FOUR

KUWAIT

Eventually we did board the jet and spent what seemed like an eternity crammed in together like sardines before we finally landed in Kuwait. The good news was that we landed at night, so the temperature was a mere eighty-five degrees; it would be well over one hundred degrees by mid-day. Remember that we had just left a mobilization site where it was below zero and many of us were "unofficially" suffering from various cold weather illnesses.

The base we occupied was overwhelmed by troops trying to move north into Iraq. This was still early in the war, and it seemed like no one in command was prepared for the movement of so many troops, especially at this base. There were extremely long lines in front of every building. This was before cell phones were available in Kuwait, so we stood in line for up to two hours to use the pay phone for a twenty minute call home. Long lines are a common feature of military life, especially in a deployed situation. The one thing that infuriated us was the fact that an American phone carrier appeared to be taking advantage of deployed troops by inflating phone card charges. The phone cards we had purchased in the United States that were worth one hundred minutes there were now worth only ten minutes overseas—a ninety percent reduction in value. We had no warning of this, and the company's answer was that we were making overseas calls on domestic cards. That may sound obvious enough except it does not take into account the peculiar situation wherein deployed troops find themselves. There was a lot of noise made about this back home and eventually adjustments were made for deployed soldiers using phone cards.

Although we made an attempt to prepare for our mission in Iraq, we really did not know what to expect so we just kept to the basics: weapons and gear maintenance, land navigation (land nav) and communication (coms) familiarization. When not training or standing in long lines, we hung out in our own "circus tent," named this due to its enormous size and circus-like stripes. It was during this down time that my faith became the subject of conversation. Soldiers would discuss the issue that faith might play for soldiers about to enter a combat zone and the possibility of death. The soldiers in my unit knew that I worked at a Christian school, so I was sought out by those who had serious questions about the reality of life and death and what that might mean for them. It also made me a target for chastisement by those who held some animosity toward Christianity.

It was at these times that I believed the Lord had sent me with this unit; I once spent as long as three hours talking with one particular soldier about his faith. My wife and kids had given me a new study Bible to take with me. It was an invaluable asset, not just for sharing the Gospel, but for my own study and prayer as well. During the time that we were "stranded" in Kuwait I was able to share my faith directly with over a dozen men and led three to the Lord prior to our departure. Yet this time spent sharing God's word did not come without my own internal conflict. I was still torn by my desire to be right before God and to enter my time in Iraq as an obedient soldier just doing his duty; I would kill the enemy as dictated by our Rules of Engagement (ROE).

Deep in my heart I still harbored a burning anger and hatred for those who had attacked us on 9/11 and anyone who would align themselves with them. I would be lying if I did not admit that I was scared about facing the enemy on their turf. My hatred had grown so deep and dark that it overwhelmed any other emotion I had at times. I was obviously conflicted and felt guilty about my attitude. I struggled and prayed, but only managed to suppress my hatred;

honestly I did not want to let go of it, because it gave me strength to overcome the fear of what lay ahead. It was as if my courage was being fueled by my anger toward our enemies. The greater my hatred grew, the more I would search out opportunities for combat hoping to kill as many of the enemy as I could.

This became a two-edged sword: I believe this attitude gave me an advantage when dealing with future hardships, but it also served to drive a wedge between me and my Savior. I have heard it said that you cannot have an honest relationship with God without dealing with the sin in your own life. My problem was not ignoring my sin but actually embracing it, rationalizing that it was keeping me alive and making me more effective with the mission before me. I brazenly told myself that I would "settle up" with God when I got home, and if I did not make it home then I was certain He would "settle up" with me.

We arrived in Kuwait with the belief that we would be transported to Iraq shortly. However, it became apparent that we had fallen through the cracks and were literally stranded. There were so many troops trying to move north that our NG Company did not have the authority necessary to secure our entire unit a flight. Most of our command finally flew out and we laughed about not having "a ride to the war." Eventually we had to fly "space available" in small groups until we all arrived at our first base in northern Iraq.

CHAPTER FIVE

KURDISTAN

The big day came when space was available and we flew to northern Iraq seated on cargo netting, wondering if the circulation in our legs would ever return. We landed at an Iraqi airport in what was formerly known as Kurdistan. The Kurds are an ethnic minority that populates the northern section of Iraq, eastern Turkey and northwestern Iran. These are the same people that Saddam Hussein used nerve agents on as a means to control them and intimidate any other groups in Iraq that were not staying in line. I remember viewing pictures of the streets of Kurdish villages lined with the dead bodies of people who suffered a horrible death at the hands of their own government.

When I saw first-hand the cruel oppression that Saddam had inflicted on his own people, I believed America did the right thing by taking him down. Although some people have asked me, "If this is true should we not invade every country ruled by an evil dictator?" I would answer, "of course not"; yet does that mean that we must never help some who are oppressed if we cannot help them all? I believe that we as individuals and as a nation can only help others when we have the courage and moral standing to do so and for no other reason.

I found this area of Iraq to be unlike what I had seen on television while in Kuwait. It was no flat infinite desert like Kuwait, but rather rolling hills covered with green grass, scattered trees and an abundance of streams and herds of animals. The area didn't have as many trees as we had in northern New England, but it still didn't feel totally foreign. The air was reasonably clear and the Kurdish people extremely polite.

We settled in at our new base with two man trailers and decent surroundings. The Kurds were good to work with; aside from dealing with the enemy, this looked to be a good tour overall. That should have been our first clue that things would change; our company eventually split up and my platoon moved south to central Iraq to the Sunni Triangle (ST), Saddam's home territory. We went from working where the locals hated Saddam and saw us as liberators from his tribal stronghold, to where the locals saw us as invaders.

THE PALACE

We were told that it was a better move because we would be living in one of Saddam's former palaces. Sure enough when we rolled in the buildings were amazing to behold; it looked like something out of a Hollywood movie about Babylon (but with bullet holes in the walls). It was then that my gunner spoke words of wisdom.

"We are not staying in any of these buildings; we're the Nasty Guard. There has got to be a ghetto here somewhere."

(Nasty Guard was an insult often casted at the National Guard by active duty soldiers because in their minds we were not professionals.) Of course my gunner was right. We drove past all the big amazing buildings, past the Post Exchange (PX), the DFAC and the recreational building (MWR) and continued down to the swamp. This area near the Tigris River was where Saddam "kept women" in a small collection of buildings next to man-made ponds that were now a dark shade of puke green. Being so close to the river meant that we were dealing with mosquitoes and the possibility of malaria.

These three buildings were once well maintained with marble floors and walls, stone carvings and gold-plated art work throughout. Spacious bedrooms with open air patios overlooked a manmade pond stocked with exotic fish. Upon our arrival the plumbing was not functioning and most of the wiring had been ripped out. What once housed maybe six women was now home to approximately forty soldiers and their gear. No one dared swim in the green ponds, but we did manage to go fishing. Using the antennas from our HMVs with string and hotdogs for bait we entertained ourselves with catch and release fishing during what little down time we had. I mentioned this activity to my family and my oldest brother Ray sent me a collapsible fishing pole with a small tackle box. It was a big hit and a lot of fun when we could fish; it is the simple things that help make difficult times pass easier.

Sometimes the best military leaders think outside the box. Due to our constant movement and reassignment our luggage was lost, meaning that most of the gear meant to sustain us for the entire year was missing. Just when we had lost hope of ever seeing our gear again, a young officer took the initiative and devised a plan to find our gear. Our gear had been loaded into a couple of metal containers called the conex back at Ft. Dix and was shipped out ahead of us. This was vital gear; For example, many of the soldiers were living with a minimal supply of uniforms. Not only was the conex not at our base waiting for us, it was nowhere to be found.

Our leader acquired the numbers that were assigned to our conexes and with a squad began to drive to each base looking for ours. When they arrived at a base and were informed of where the conexes were stored, he would walk up and down row upon row looking for the matching numbers. Eventually he did indeed find them and our gear was returned; that is a great example of a leader taking care of the troops even when it endangered his own life by going outside the wire or outside the base.

Just when we thought things here could not get any more bizarre, we were advised by the Permanent Party (PP) of the base to not walk around at night because tigers, hyenas and other wild animals were living in the tall grass near the river. It seems that Saddam kept these animals in a zoo on his palace compound. When the invasion began he set these animals loose in the hopes of creating more chaos. I had to see this zoo for myself, and what I found was not only sickening but certainly helped to confirm in my own mind that Saddam and his followers were themselves animals. The cages were indeed open and empty, but on the concrete floor were obvious blood stains from times when Saddam had thrown in live victims. We were told by a team that disassembled the cages that Saddam routinely threw his political enemies into the animal cages and made their families watch with him as they were torn to pieces and eaten. This would not be the last time I would see hard evidence that the Iraqi people survived under a living nightmare.

Occasionally we would provide convoy security for prisoner transport or detainee release. We all hated this work; handling prisoners was always more dangerous due to the nature of the work. Some of the detained Iraqis were just in the wrong place at the wrong time, and had been cleared by our Military Intelligence (MI) so we could transport them to their hometown or village for release. Others were bad news; these were Saddam's loyal soldiers who had enjoyed a certain amount of power. Their power came as an extension of their position within Saddam's regime. Iraqis do not see each other as fellow countrymen but as belonging to a particular tribe and followers of a certain Islamic tradition. Therefore all that matters to them is what tribe you belong to and whether or not you are in power.

When we loaded and unloaded detainees from the trucks, we did so one at a time. We conducted them in a very rough manner, not abusively, but in a way so that they understood we meant business. They had to believe that if they screwed with us we would kill them. If I have learned nothing else from living in the Middle East it is this: strength and the willingness to use it is all that matters to some people. If they do not fear you, you will die. Osama himself stated that America was a "Paper Tiger" and he was therefore prepared to attack us knowing that he had nothing to fear from us.

One event that I was honored to take part in was the posting of our unit guidon. A guidon is a unit flag that is posted outside of the command center for each unit. I got to hold the actual guidon that was carried to the Pacific Theater during World War II. It was donated to our unit prior to our deployment so we could carry it to Iraq and post it alongside our current guidon.

CHAPTER SIX

MISSIONS TO SAVE GILLIGAN

The best part of being based at Saddam's former palace was the fact that we did not spend a lot of time there; rather we were on the road performing convoy escort (CE) missions which could last for days. Most of our missions became known as "Missions to Save Gilligan." We would be sent out for a short escort to a nearby base and upon arrival be advised that we were then to escort another convoy onto another base and so on. What started out as a "three-hour tour" became a never ending series of CEs that could last for days.

The first time this happened it caught us by surprise. We were not prepared for such a lengthy mission. From that point forward our squad was prepared for almost any crazy order that came down to us. We would meet up with the convoy leader at a designated base, discuss logistics, routes of travel, ROEs and proceed to the next base which usually took all day.

I discovered that I preferred to spend my tour traveling from base to base rather than just sitting back at our own. Most soldiers will tell you they would rather be as far away from the "Flag Pole" (away from their CoC) as possible.

TAKING FIRE

During my first tour to Iraq I had opportunities to engage the enemy on their ground. Due to our CE missions my unit was ambushed on a regular basis. Once I got over the initial shock of being shot at I responded with a vengeance. While some soldiers were hoping that we would get through each mission with no attacks, I was praying just the opposite. I realized that when the enemy shot at me I discovered his exact position (there is an old saying with the infantry, "tracers work both ways"). I wanted my time in Iraq to count for something. I did not come here as a tourist, and I wanted to return home with the knowledge that I had damaged the enemy and protected my family in the only way I could. This outlook reminded me of a scene from the movie *Pearl Harbor* (Bay, 2001) when Ben Affleck's character volunteered to fly for the British Royal Air Force (RAF). He was asked by a British aviator if Affleck was in a hurry to die, and Affleck responded with "I'm in a hurry to matter."

Our CE missions were comprised of hours of driving around Iraq staring at miles of sand, camels and mud huts with satellite dishes on the roof. I even saw a number of nomadic tribes that had satellite dishes mounted outside their tents. This was an amazing picture of a mixture of old world traditions and new world technology. It was also a testament to how things had changed for Iraqis since our toppling of Saddam's regime. Prior to the American invasion it was illegal to own a satellite dish because Saddam wanted to control the flow of information in and out of his country. Now they were everywhere.

When we first arrived in Iraq we were briefed by the soldiers we were replacing. They warned us about being ambushed. They stated that when you are forced to stop in a city, listen to the "call to prayer" that comes from the mosque (technically over a loudspeaker projected from the tower next to the mosque, a minaret). The call to prayer is sent out at specific times of the day and of course is in Arabic. Correctly assuming that most American soldiers do not speak Arabic, the enemy would use the loud speakers to announce and coordinate attacks on us. Being aware of the time of day and what the call normally sounds like allowed us to prepare for such an attack; however, however it became routine that if our convoy was forced to stop that we were about to get hit with enemy fire.

This was just another incident where I was appalled and felt like I was in the *Twilight Zone*. The enemy would use mosques as a means of attacking us, while hiding inside of them, knowing that we were forbidden to enter or fire at any Muslim religious building. What kind of people use the pretext of "holy ground" as an excuse for protection while trying to kill someone else? This would be similar to me shooting from the steeple of my Baptist church back home, knowing that my enemy could not fire back or enter my sanctuary. This also fueled my contempt for my enemy. Yet I was only scratching the surface of what I would witness later.

This would not be the last time I would be disgusted by the low level tactics they would use. Throughout my tours mosques were used to announce attacks, as staging areas, as actual headquarters and as a place to take prisoners for torture. Imagine dragging someone inside of your church, tying them down and drilling holes through their kneecaps (which are a common method of torture with our enemies).

I asked the officer who was briefing us why we didn't eliminate their advantage by either firing on mosques or going in after them. By not doing this we are setting ourselves up for failure and the war will unnecessarily drag on if we are intent on not offending the people who are trying to kill us. His answer was that the United States did not want to antagonize other Muslims by doing this, my answer to him was "then why are the friendly Muslims not outraged by others using their mosques this way?" He stated that they most likely are outraged, but the average Iraqi has been so beaten down by Saddam that they fear to take a stand for anything. (During my later tour in Afghanistan I witnessed a very different reaction by the Afghan National Army (ANA). The enemy rarely used mosques as a fortress because the ANA would go in after them and drag them out by their heels.)

When we discussed these events at night most of our soldiers were horrified by what they saw and learned of our enemy. Yet there was always a critic of Christianity who would snidely accuse Christians of the same horrors, using the Inquisition and other terrible actions by the medieval Christian Church. I would respond by thanking them for proving my point; they had to draw from medieval history in order to make the comparison to "modern day" Islam. I would then ask them to imagine the Christian church without the Renaissance, without the Reformation and without the Enlightenment. "What then would we have?" I asked. "Islam," he answered.

We were also advised that if you saw a news reporter with a camera, get ready, you were about to be in an ambush. It seems that the enemy was feeding their plans to various news agencies. This was done in order to maximize their propaganda opportunities and the news agency would get live coverage of Americans in combat. Unbelievable as that sounds it happened to us just that way. Once, our convoy was forced to stop in Baghdad with two- and three- story buildings on either side of the road. We exited our trucks and took cover while watching the windows and roof tops for any suspicious movement.

It was then that a blonde-haired woman with a microphone accompanied by a cameraman exited a building adjacent to our truck. There were no identifying markers on their equipment but I could hear the woman clearly speaking English. Within seconds of their appearance bullets began pinging off the side of our trucks from the building the newscaster had her back to. I was stunned for a moment; this news crew (American or otherwise) knew that American soldiers were going to be ambushed. They allowed it to happen, knowing that soldiers could die. Later that night as that picture raced through my mind over and over, I became sick asking myself why they were there. Was it just to get a sensational video or some twisted anti-war news agenda or both? How does someone rationalize their way through something like this? That was one of the most demoralizing moments of my time in Iraq; the thought that newscasters would knowingly be a part of an ambush. It sticks in my gut to this day.

As we continued to take fire I was trying to determine the actual location of the enemy shooters. The shots started from the right but quickly stopped and began coming from the buildings on the left side of the street. The combination of seeing the news team along with the fact that someone was shooting at my brothers angered me like nothing before. The anger I felt was not some type of out-of-control rage, it was much deeper than that. It grounded me and I felt almost invincible. I immediately began shouting orders to soldiers with the convoy trucks behind my own, directing their fire and looking for targets of opportunity myself.

It was then that I noticed that the pinging sound of bullets striking metal was all too close. Bullets were striking the side of our truck; the enemy had targeted me and was walking the rounds in. I jumped behind my HMV door for some protection and scanned the rooftops in the direction that the shots had come from. Just then I saw him, a man popped up over the short wall on a roof top approximately two hundred yards out on the second floor. He fired his AK-47 at me in a spraying motion and then disappeared behind the wall when he knew I had seen him and he was no longer willing to take the time to aim. Firing a semiautomatic rifle in a spraying motion, especially at that range, is extremely inaccurate.

I rested my M16 on top of the door and placed my sights near the rooftop where I had last seen him. Sure enough he popped up again, fired another burst of rounds, and disappeared. The whole world became still. I focused in on that one moment with my sights trained at his last location. Like clockwork, he popped up for another volley in the same location and I fired a three round burst at the silhouette of his head. His entire body was jerked backwards so violently that his head snapped up toward the sky and his arms opened up while he retained a death grip on his rifle, spraying bullets as he fell. A soldier nearby had seen and heard what had happened, called my name and gave me a thumbs up. At that very moment I did not even begin to think about what I had just done. We were still under fire and I had moved onto my next target.

The enemy intensified its attack with small arms and RPGs, so I moved to the side of a five-ton (a large truck used to carry troops and or supplies). There was a soldier from the convoy we were escorting manning a machine gun in their turret. Due to the advantage of his higher position I asked what he could see. Before he could answer I saw a shocked look on his face as I caught the boom of an RPG being fired behind me. An instant later the grenade from that RPG impacted the metal door of the truck within inches of my head! I was frozen there in time waiting for the inevitable blast that would kill me, but it never came. When the paralysis of the moment subsided I saw why I was still alive. The RPG was either not armed or had malfunctioned, which was not uncommon.

I looked up and noticed the gunners face was still pale from shock then he suddenly broke out laughing and pointed over my shoulder. I turned around to see the enemy who had fired at us standing on a rooftop still holding the empty launcher being slapped across the head by another enemy soldier; it looked like a something out of a Three Stooges movie. While we were laughing the gunner exclaimed, "Hey shouldn't we be shooting at them?" I replied, "they will most likely kill themselves before the week is out." Within a second of my remark they were out of sight.

I then heard the call to mount up and move out, it appeared this ambush was over and the road ahead of us was open. One of the guys from my squad saw the RPG round in the truck door and exclaimed, "SSG Moore you have got to be the luckiest soldier in Iraq!"

I replied with, "I would rather believe that I am blessed."

Another soldier who was a bit of a comedian stated, "Yea, Moore's a Christian he's got a guardian angel."

"That's cool," stated the first soldier, "maybe I should ride with you; what's your angel's name?"

The comedian then jumped in with, "Legion, for we are many!" causing all of us to break out in much needed laughter.

CHAPTER SEVEN

HUMAN SHIELDS

Our missions to "save Gilligan" continued with regularity, which again was better than being back at our base. We would escort convoys from one base to another, sometimes sleeping in tents and eating a hot meal in the DFAC, other times it was MREs and sleeping on top of our truck under the open sky. We knew we could depend on each other for whatever happened, regardless of the fact that we were following orders. We were removed enough to feel like masters of our own destinies.

Nevertheless, the enemy had really stepped up the attacks and, at the same time, had reached a new low, at least for me. To cite an example of the amazing lack of courage of our enemies, they announced that they had a leader in a man named Sadr (the namesake of Sadr City, the ghetto section of Baghdad). Sadr had declared war on the infidel Americans and announced that his "army" wore a black uniform with a green sash. Perfect! By doing this they identified themselves as enemy combatants as well as their specific uniform. Therefore, our new ROE stated that we could engage anyone wearing those colors on sight. When we did see men in these uniforms they were already shooting at us but it definitely made our job a lot easier and engage the enemy we did. This lasted a few short weeks until they realized the folly of openly identifying themselves as the enemy and ceased wearing such uniforms and returned to hiding amongst the common people.

This did not surprise me, as I had come to realize that our enemy were only brave when shooting from the rooftops or hiding in mosques. Yet my Iraq tour had reached another gut-wrenching low point when we encountered the strategy of "human shields." We were briefed that the enemy were trying a new tactic during ambushes: shooting at us from the rooftops and through open windows while actually standing behind women and children! I had to see it to believe it, which did not take very long.

Our ROE was very specific and practical. We were to engage the enemy with controlled fire at specific targets of opportunity taking every precaution to not cause collateral damage to the human shields. This may sound callous at first but the intent was clear and the reasoning sound. The enemy believed that American soldiers would not return fire for fear of injuring the non-combatants, which would allow them to shoot at us unhindered. By not returning fire not only would our own soldiers most likely be injured, but the human shields might as well due to collateral damage. I honestly believe the enemy was hoping for that type of collateral damage.

In the previously mentioned situation with the news reporter being forewarned of the enemy's future attack, they obviously wanted the press, especially bad press. This tactic would make Americans back home become overwhelmed with the burden of seeing their own soldiers being injured and even killed. It was much like the way the Viet Cong used the American media to promote their own narrative. Basically, if the enemy thinks this ploy works they will continue to use it. Therefore, we had to take that advantage away from our enemy.

It was another trip through Baghdad when our convoy was forced to stop. We exited the trucks and scanned the buildings for any possible aggressive action. I saw someone moving toward us down a narrow alleyway, it was two men dragging a women and a small girl both of whom were screaming and trying to get free. Before we could consider any course of action they entered the building and were out of sight. The two men then appeared in separate open windows, each holding a human shield in front of them. The man at the left window held the woman with her arms behind her back as he raised his AK-47, preparing to fire. The other man had a similar stance, except he held the young girl with his arm around her throat. Both hostages looked terrified and were crying.

I was in shock at what I witnessed. I could not bring myself to believe that they were actually going to use these innocent people as shields. A soldier standing next to me asked "what the hell are they doing?" Before I could think of an answer I realized we had stood still for far too long and that the enemy had seen us. They opened fire in our direction, and we both took cover behind our trucks, trying to decide what course of action to take. I became enraged but was grounded enough that I remained concerned for the safety of my buddies and our convoy, so I did not act irrationally.

These men were using a woman and a child for cover, and I wanted these cowardly men dead. We would not leave until those hostages were free and the enemy was dead. Our ROE gave us the go to engage the enemy in this situation, but with extreme caution. I took up a supported position along the back of my truck and tried to get a clear shot at the man on the right who was holding the girl. He must have thought, "these Americans will not shoot back," because he was standing in such a fashion that his head and right shoulder were visible.

I aimed at his left eye hoping a clean head shot would drop him instantly and the girl could possibly get out of the house. Before I could fire, the girl began to struggle and they were both moving back and forth too much for me to get a clear shot. I decided on suppressive fire, if I could not hit him I could keep his head down and thus prevent him from firing at us. I fired one round at the window frame just to the side of his right eye. Those buildings are made of dried mud so my shot was effective; it struck the side of the window causing the mud brick and wood to shatter, creating the desired effect. The spray of mud chips next to his face caused him to jump back and I lost sight of the two of them.

It was then that I noticed that other soldiers were employing the same tactic as I had and were laying suppressive fire at the other window frame. When attacks like this take place our SOP dictates that we radio the Quick Response Force (QRF or Sheriff) assigned to that Area of Operation (AO) for assistance. They had just arrived and were entering the building just as we received orders to mount up and move out. I was advised later that both of the hostages were fine and the enemy had been taken out by the QRF.

When we had arrived at our next base we followed our usual SOPs of vehicle/gear/weapons maintenance, hygiene, food and finally sleep. While I lay on my cot staring up at the stars I began to review what had transpired that day. My hands began to shake; the reality of what I had witnessed had finally caught up with me. The thought that these cowards had purposely placed a woman and a child in harm's way was the lowest thing I had ever seen. What if I had injured that little girl? I would not be able to get past that, even though they placed her in harm's way deliberately. These were supposedly brave Muslim Jihadists fighting for Allah against the evil infidels. They were lower than cowards; these were animals, at least in my estimation at that time. This incident and others like it only served to cement my anger for, hatred of and absolute contempt for these people that have turned a generation of young men and women seeking spiritual enlightenment into cold blooded killers. From that point on every man I killed was one less flying a plane into a building or using children as shields; I thought the world would spin easier every time I pulled the trigger.

CHAPTER EIGHT

ON THE LIGHTER SIDE

Despite what we see on TV, war-like law enforcement is more hurry up and wait than the constant action the movies might portray. Like life there are humorous times to look back on and laugh, if for no other reason than to help keep us sane, at least for a time. I think about situations that are hard to either believe or laugh at unless you were there but I will try. I want to share some of these stories for a few reasons, to demonstrate that war is not constant combat and that life happens no matter where you are or who you are with.

There had been a tremendous amount of action lately, and our convoy had arrived at its destination only to be advised that there was no room at the inn. The enemy had effectively shut down many of the normal routes convoys traveled so the obvious effect was a traffic jam of enormous proportions. Our convoy, along with countless others, had to park outside the base on the four lane highway rather than inside behind tall concrete walls with tower guards. The base PP did provide some security but we also organized some of our own realizing that we were presenting a target rich environment.

We settled in as best we could for a few days of hurry up and wait. By this time we had been on the road for a week, riding in our trucks and choking on dust with the outside temperature well over one hundred degrees every day. We did our best to keep our critical body parts clean but at this point my body odor could have choked a camel. I decided to take a shower using two large water bottles that I left out on top of my truck to warm in the sun. There were no shower facilities for us outside the base and we were literally parked on the second lane of a four lane highway with trucks of all sizes as far as the eye could see.

I decided to wait until dark when all of the other soldiers were sleeping to attempt my quick field shower. Finally it was dark, all of the lights from the trucks were off, and I could not hear anyone talking or moving around. I placed a piece of cardboard on the ground in the median between the four lanes and rapidly undressed. I rinsed myself down and began to wash when I heard a soldier call my name.

"SSG Moore, is that you? What are you doing?!"

"I'm taking a shower. Now shut up and go back to sleep," I stated trying to give an order without raising my voice.

Having a sense of humor he decided that everyone out there should enjoy the fact that I was bathing in the open and turned on the headlights of our truck directed at me. Well that did the trick. In an instant I could hear people talking and then laughter combined with the sound of horns blowing and even the hoots and whistles of the female soldiers. Standing there buck naked still covered with soap, I realized there was no sense in stopping what I had begun and continued to wash and rinse. That only served to encourage the comments which began to sound more like cat calls at a strip club. The next day several soldiers stopped by to thank me for the previous night's entertainment, and a few female soldiers even jokingly handed me one dollar bills. I was embarrassed but I also felt like a new man since I no longer smelled like a dead horse. Spending time in a combat environment you quickly learn that some of the protocols of polite society need to be ignored, so just laugh it off and move on.

Another humorous event, at least after the fact, occurred during a detainee transport and release convoy mission. We had been ordered to pick up a large number of detainees slotted for release at a nearby base and to drop them off at their respective towns. When we began to load them into our vehicle we realized we had a problem; our interpreter would not be traveling with us and we needed to make three different drops at towns across the area.

"How do we know who gets off where?" someone asked.

One of the guys came up with an idea. As we loaded each Iraqi the interpreter asked him what his hometown was and if we could write the first letter of that town on his forehead. No detainee had a problem with this idea, they were just thrilled to be on their way home. We took a sharpie and wrote the first letter of each of their hometowns on their foreheads, that way we would know who got off at each location.

This plan worked like a charm at our first stop. We even loaded the Iraqis into the trucks in the reverse order of their release. However the next stop was a different story. We did not know it at that time but that particular city had a reputation for being a wild place. Meaning that Iraqi men could engage in all sorts of behavior that was forbidden in the Koran. Did I mention that our government had paid each of these men cash to compensate them for their time while incarcerated? Once they realized where they were the trucks emptied completely in minutes and men began running down the street away from us. Our first reaction was to try and stop them until the SGT in charge stated, "Hey these guys are being released, so we have no obligation to hold them. If they want out here that's up to them. Let's go home." We loaded our trucks and hit the road, headed back to our base feeling rather good about getting the job done early for a change and possibly returning in time for a hot meal.

The next day we heard of a disturbance in the city where we had dropped off the detainees, it seemed there were reports of a sudden influx of men with money to burn in that city. Apparently they had become drunk (yes some Muslims drink alcohol) and disorderly. It did not take a genius to realize what had happened, yet we were never questioned about our mission to that city, so we just chalked it up for experience and laughs.

CHAPTER NINE

THE RED CROSS

We had spent a few days back at our base at the palace awaiting our order to mount up and pick up another convoy when the 1st SGT drove up and pulled me to the side. He looked concerned so I knew something was not right. He stated that they had received a notification from the Red Cross (RC) that I had a family emergency back home. He did not have any details; the Red Cross would only release that information to me directly.

The RC serves as one of the few ways a soldier's family may contact him during an emergency. Family members contact the RC directly with the specific details of the family crisis and the RC then has the ability to verify the stated crisis and contact the soldier's CoC, even in Iraq. Many times an RC notification means a death in the family, so I was obviously upset and was immediately relieved of my duties and taken back to our HQ to call home.

I spoke with my wife and the good news was that no one had died or was in critical condition. However, there was still a serious problem with my family. My youngest son was becoming traumatized by my absence. He is autistic, and while I was away he became depressed and could not sleep at night due to night terrors that kept him and my wife distressed. She had taken him to see a doctor who said that my son believed I was literally fighting in a war zone that wouldn't end. The doctor likened it to living through the movie *Black Hawk Down* (Scott, 2001) day after day, and said that it was too much for him to handle. The doctor was concerned that if I did not come home soon and let my son see me alive that he may need to be hospitalized for treatment. My CoC followed SOPs and I was packing to leave for home within a few days. While most of the soldiers were very supportive, a few made it known that they thought that I was somehow making this up and going home because I "could not hack it," or that I was actually a coward. Those accusations, no matter how inaccurate, burned deep inside of my heart and I was to pay a price for adding them to my already conflicted spirit. Nevertheless, I was soon home taking care of my son, with my family and friends, and away from the war, at least for a little while.

CHAPTER TEN

I Didn't See That Coming!

It was around this time that I began to reflect on what God had done in my life and how He was working on my heart even when I did not realize it. I have shared all the different reasons that I decided to deploy to Iraq, from patriotism to honor, and even to the less noble motivation of revenge masked as righteous judgment. I discussed my struggle with my burning desire to kill the enemy far beyond what was required.

What I did not see coming was just how God was going to intervene in my life when I actually thought that I was in control and that I could decide when and where He would be "allowed" to be involved with my life and those around me. How He used my status as a Christian teacher to be an open door for those who were searching for answers that the secular world could not provide. I became a safety net for those soldiers that were either unaware of the life altering experiences that were ahead of them or that they just chose to ignore out of pride or fear. God did this knowing full well that I would either have to completely walk away from my faith or that out of my desire to share God's love for all people I would submit to

Him. I would become a willing servant to the Holy Spirit attempting to comfort any that came to me with heavy hearts.

God also began to work on my perception of Muslim people and my feelings toward them in general. Nothing will reach the heart of every soldier like a child, especially a child in need. While in Iraq I consistently saw children that I did not recognize as Muslims but only as children. I became aware of children who were in dire situations, who were obviously malnourished and homeless. There were children that would run out to wave at our convoys giving us thumbs up, a big smile and ask for candy.

When I interacted with these children I realized that they were just like those back home, but what I failed to realize was that these kids would someday become Muslim adults. Would I hate them then or just find a way to separate the two groups through rationalization? What God made clear to me at the end of this tour was that these kids, like their parents, needed a Savior just as much as I did. I had to search my heart and face the fact that my hate would have allowed me to deny any opportunity to share the Gospel in deed or word. I had accepted the fact that my desire was for them to die and Hell was something they deserved.

I was most definitely convicted by the Holy Spirit to recognize my mindset and own the fact that I was in sin. I prayed for forgiveness, asked for a softer heart and that I would see all people as needing God's salvation through Christ regardless of my perception of any wrong done toward me or mine. I felt satisfied at that moment that I was right with God and that the darkness that had fallen over my heart had been lifted. It would not be until my last tour that I would realize just how deep some scars go and that it would take being on deaths door to force me to face the truth of what was truly buried beneath.

SECTION III

Chapter Eleven

The Homecoming

Initially it was good to be home with my wife and family, especially to attend to my son's distress. We met with his doctor and it was obvious that our effort to help my son would take longer than a few weeks. I was told by the NG that for me to stay home longer I would need to file for a hardship discharge. That sounded rather drastic at that time but after seeing how distraught my son and wife had become over my absence I felt a tremendous burden to do whatever I had to help them.

I filed the appropriate paperwork, met with numerous people and within a short period of time I was not only out of Iraq, but also out of the Army NG entirely. Over a period of a few weeks we made great progress with my son's problems and my family was back on solid ground. It was summer when I returned so school was not in session, which may have made things worse for me personally. I now had too much time on my hands to spend thinking about all of my issues, including those that had begun prior to going to Iraq and those that had arisen while I was there. The biggest issue I had was guilt. I developed a sense of embarrassment for leaving Iraq early, even though I knew I had legitimate reasons for it. I could not get past having left my buddies back there.

I became depressed, withdrawn and irritable about the entire subject. What I did not realize at that time was I was also suffering from the early stages of Post-Traumatic Stress Disorder (PTSD). It was during one of those tough days that my wife came to me with the phone and suggested that I call the NG and ask to re-enlist and to return to Iraq. I was obviously shocked by her statement. I thought she was glad that I was home and our son was doing so much better now. All that was true, but as she put it, "What good does it do us if you're not here [mentally] with us? I am afraid that you'll grow bitter and resent us for having to come home." I assured her that I did not feel that way, yet she insisted that I at least try. She said if it did not work then we knew it was not meant to be and we could move on; otherwise we might drag those issues around with us forever.

As much as I protested her thoughts on our situation I knew she was right. She had been more insightful about what was happening to us. Even though I had not talked to her about how I was feeling, she could read me like a book and I could not argue her point. I contacted my prior unit's CoC about going back to Iraq, specifically being reassigned back to my old unit at the Palace. The responses I got ranged from casual indifference to a resounding "No way!" Whether it was because of the paperwork involved or that they were certain that I had not left for the right reasons they were not only refusing my return but would fight it however they could.

After numerous trips to state HQs I did meet an officer who took the time to talk with me about my case. After explaining my situation and my desire to return to Iraq and finish my tour honorably he consented to help. I took the re-enlistment oath right in my own living room and I was assigned to his unit. Try as he might I was stalled from getting back to my unit until it was finally too late to go because they would be home in a few months anyway. The conflict I felt was now tearing me apart. I began to question my reasons for coming home, how to deal with my anger toward our enemy and how to come to terms with all that I had seen and done, especially as a Christian.

I decided that all of these questions could only be answered by deploying again to any theater of action. I then did something that any smart soldier rarely does—I volunteered to go anywhere as long

as it was to a combat zone. I did not think it was a blessing at the time, but God answered my request with Afghanistan. Our state NG did not have a unit deploying to Afghanistan at that time, so I was attached to a training unit that was mobilizing out of Ft. Hood, Texas. It was not actually just one unit, but a conglomeration of soldiers from approximately twenty-seven different states all coming together to form a training unit based on their skill sets. My skill set having been formerly mountain infantry qualified made me a good bet for the rugged terrain of Afghanistan. The announcement of my redeploying went over like a lead balloon, especially with my extended family. Over time they realized that it was a done deal and they would support me in any way they could.

CHAPTER TWELVE

FORT HOOD

The first indication that this was going to be a very different tour was my send off, or should I say the lack of one. My first tour was marked by a large gathering of family, friends, military personnel and politicians. Some had come to wish us well and show their support for the troops, while others appeared for nothing more than a photo op for their constituency, but I will avoid politics as much as I can at least for now.

I arrived at Ft. Hood with approximately two hundred and fifty soldiers from various state NG units and reserve units as well. Eventually we were broken down into teams of eighteen soldiers; half being officers and the other half being NCOs. The idea behind these teams was that we would deploy to Afghanistan as a team, NCOs with officers for the best effect for each Afghan unit. After approximately two months of mobilization training we would be wheels up for Afghanistan. Unfortunately most of the training, like before, was a waste of time.

We were going through basic soldier skills training; we were all officers and NCOs, so by its nature that was entirely unnecessary. We also spent endless hours subjected to "death by PowerPoint" briefings where we were indoctrinated into the politically correct version of Islam. I believe the misinformation that was disseminated in these meetings to the troops over the years did more damage than good for all concerned.

Nothing much had changed since my original mobilization out of Ft. Dix other than the weather. The useful portions of mobilization like weapons qualification, gear issue, medical and personnel updates could have been accomplished within a two-week span of time. Yet the greatest benefit of our time at Ft. Hood was getting to know the other members of our team, "The War Eagles." I have to say that this was the greatest combination of talent, skill, experience and leadership I have experienced before or since. Everyone on the team brought something of value to the table and complemented the rest of the team. I especially appreciated the relaxed attitude toward rank within our team. Not that we did not extend proper military protocol, but an eighteen-man team of experienced soldiers is not looking to impress anyone else as well as the fact that we are all depending on each other and working together side by side. The very real sense of brotherhood came to life during this tour and I have not been entirely able to experience it at that level since.

Just prior to our departure we were informed that our team was being broken apart and dispersed to various parts of Afghanistan. This was unsettling for me because I had come to appreciate working with these men. I also knew that I could count on any one of them to watch my back. Worst of all was the realization that I would have to establish myself with an entirely new team, which I thought would not work as well as the current team. Another uncertainty was our final destination and mission, which kept changing. I learned to appreciate the adage "when your boots hit the sand, there you are."

My time at Ft. Hood was not without the added stress of worrying about my family. Would they fare better during this tour than the last one? Second guessing my decision to redeploy was a frequent issue that gnawed at me when issues arose at home. The closer I got to actually deploying the more I became SFC Moore and began to get my head into the game, which also meant revisiting old feelings of fear, anger and hatred for our enemy. Once again, I welcomed many of these feeling because I believed that they made me a more effective soldier.

"A distracted soldier is a dead soldier," and I would not be distracted! I was determined to be an effective, focused soldier and leader. I began to visualize what Afghanistan might be like. Would the people be just like the Muslims I met in Iraq? Would I be placed in a dangerous mission with the enemy trying to kill me again? Deep down I hoped for it. I had already experienced something that became very evident later on—if the enemy shoots at you, you can shoot back! I don't mean to sound like an insensitive killer but we were at war; these people killed my countrymen and tried to kill my son.

CHAPTER THIRTEEN

KABUL

We flew out in the middle of winter, stopping in New York City; Shannon, Ireland; Turkey; and finally Kirgizstan on our way to Afghanistan. After a few days in Kirgizstan we made the long, cold flight over the mountains of Afghanistan to land in the capital city of Kabul. We were transported across the city to the base which would serve as our staging area for our eventual FOBs. This base, we soon learned, was an okay place to visit for the PX and food, but was literally "the Flag Pole."

The command of our entire task force was based here and included too many officers and senior NCOs with too much rank and nothing relevant to do. There were people who spent their time shopping at the bazaars purchasing Afghan rugs at reduced prices for shipment home for resale. The good thing about these leaders was that they generally left us alone; it was those that were placed in charge of something totally irrelevant that had little or no bearing on the greater mission at hand that made life miserable.

A perfect example of this fact was that our request for night vision goggles, a rather critical piece of equipment for war fighting at night, was denied. The stated reason was that our mission did not call for them because we were only training Afghan soldiers and should not be out at night. The more accurate reason was multi-layered. The command in some cases did not understand our mission. They also did not want to give up these sensitive items for fear that we were incapable of keeping them safe. The final reason was something that I learned of firsthand several times. "Soldier envy," is a casual expression used commonly by the SF, meant that there were many in command who were envious of our ability to go out with the Afghans. To have the freedom to get away from the command, run our own missions without requesting permission at every turn and quite possibly see enough action to be awarded a commendation of some type.

Unfortunately, I would run into this issue again. Some leaders did not understand that we were at war and were only interested in their own careers, regardless of the impact on their subordinates or the mission. The justification for keeping the night vision goggles on the base and not out on mission, was that they were used by officers who walked the base at night looking for soldiers engaged in prohibited sexual activity.

This frustration quickly rose to anger when we were ordered to become pay and contract officers. These positions are held by "officers" who negotiate contracts with local nationals and other non-military entities for goods and services that cannot be supplied through normal methods, such as buying food and fuel to sustain the ANA that we were working with, or even funding building projects like well pumps for clean drinking water.

Soldiers are used to taking orders, even foolish ones. We were ordered to do an officer's job because they were either too afraid to go outside the wire and/or because it would take them out of their comfortable surroundings on the base. To add insult to injury, we were required to sign for approximately fifty thousand dollars in cash once per month. When we returned to base we had to produce signed receipts with a spread sheet tabulating every transaction down to the dollar. They were treating this like we were back in the United States dealing with any American sub-contractor.

We attempted to explain that we were not equipped for this type of an accounting mission. Our command ignored the fact that most Afghans are illiterate and make all deals with a handshake. We were told that we were going to do it anyway and that if we did not have receipts for every dollar spent we would go to prison. Later we were advised by the soldiers we were replacing of how to meet these unrealistic requirements. They would record every transaction on a spreadsheet they had developed, and the interpreters would hand write the receipts and sign them themselves. We soon learned that the only thing that mattered with some in command was the paperwork; if the paperwork was good then we were good to go. So we counted and signed for our fifty thousand dollars and headed off for our primary FOB. (Just so there is no question, every dollar was accounted for within my team. Every dollar!)

In fairness to the officers and senior NCOs that I served with, I could fill entire chapters of examples of those that went above and beyond their required duties. One such officer was Captain (CPT) Casey, a reservist who had a similar background to mine in regards to law enforcement experience, age and family. We hit it off immediately, especially since we both had respect for each other and we were very willing to rely on each other for guidance, suggestions and constructive criticism. I always knew CPT Casey had my back, and he knew that I had his; that is no small thing in a combat zone.

MAJOR WARD: AN EXAMPLE OF WHAT GOOD LEADERSHIP LOOKS LIKE.

CHAPTER FOURTEEN

YELLOW DOG

Our first impression of our new base, Yellow Dog was not good. It was a very small FOB, so small it did not even have a PX, just a chow hall, maintenance and living quarters. It is not an exaggeration to say that its dimensions were that of a football field. Yet we soon discovered that this was the best kept secret in the Stan. Due to its austere living conditions irrelevant command types (ICT) were scarce which meant that most of the soldiers there, regardless of rank, wanted to be there and understood the mission to include senior leadership.

YD was where we would stage all of our "Long Walks" (LW), a code term that I used to inform my wife that I was going outside the wire for an extended period of time and not to worry if she did not hear from me. Due to OPSEC I never told her where we were going or why. Yet Raquel understood that not hearing from me was okay as long as the chaplain did not show up at our house. My wife had a few strategies for not becoming consumed with worry for my safety. One was to avoid watching the news as it related to the war on terror, especially since most of the mainstream media had decided to exaggerate any bad news and avoid reporting the good. Another strategy was to focus on our children and to try to maintain a sense of normalcy in their lives.

Training the ANA in the use of armored vehicles.

EMBEDDED WITH THE ANA

The more things change the more they stay the same, and this was true with the Army in that you could count on your orders morphing into something you never expected. I arrived in Afghanistan preparing to train Afghan recruits in a boot camp scenario. What I stepped into was much more. I had arrived here with CPT Casey from our original Ft. Hood "War Eagles," and he and I were led out of YD and into the ANA base where I saw more armed Muslims in one place than I had ever seen before. I will admit I was flooded with a mix of emotions from fear to anger and confusion. What were we doing in the middle of all these Muslim soldiers? Was this safe?

Our mission was simply this: we were to become embedded advisors (ETT) to the ANA, which meant working and even living with them every day, including off base. I immediately protested to those who were preparing us for this tour. I explained that I had already served in Iraq and was well acquainted with Muslims. I knew that they could not be trusted to fight when we needed them to and worse they will sell us to the enemy the first chance they get. While in Iraq we would never leave a few soldiers alone in the care of Iraqi Muslims, which was SOP.

I was advised by our transition team that the Afghans were not Arabs and that they are a very different type of Muslim; these men were raised in a warrior culture. Getting them to stand and fight was not the problem—trying to maintain command and control of them when the shooting started was. They were all too eager to engage the enemy. The next point they made was hard to believe at first but I ultimately saw it played out several times during my tour in Afghanistan: their sense of honor and hospitality. I was considered a guest and would be treated as such by the Afghan soldiers and by the civilian population as well. Since CPT Casey and I had been assigned to this particular ANA Company, they were responsible for our safety and it would mean dishonor for them if something happened to either of us.

CPT Casey and I became close friends and looked out for each other through good times and bad. This relationship of fellow soldiers working together was not unique to him and me. Many of the embedded teams interacted this way, primarily out of necessity but also because it just made sense. Occasionally a team would arrive that did not grasp this concept, which caused their time in Afghanistan to be miserable and the mission to suffer.

We spent the first few weeks getting acclimated to not only the climate but more importantly the elevation. Afghanistan is called "the roof of the world" for a good reason. Much of its landscape looks like the Rocky Mountains, and it is part of the Himalayan mountain range. I was in good physical condition for my age (forty-five) but when we began foot patrols through the mountains I felt like I had been a smoker for thirty years. The thin oxygen levels were unbelievable. After only a short climb I was sucking wind and the muscle fatigue was even worse. Over time I did acclimate physically to the elevation, and I was amazed at how far I could climb without getting winded.

This also led us to another decision about our issued gear. We were required to wear all of the ridiculous body armor that the Army was issuing to soldiers for protection from Improvised Explosive Devices (IED). I say ridiculous because all soldiers were required to wear it regardless of mission demands. Wearing body armor became an issue early in our conflict in Iraq due to the enemies' deployment of IEDs. These explosives would be detonated electronically on passing United States military vehicles, either destroying the vehicles entirely or ripping a hole through the passenger compartment. The military's attempts at keeping soldiers safe had become counterproductive because when a soldier is wearing so much heavy protective armor he can barely move.

Soldiers, especially those who are trained for direct combat, realize the danger they place themselves in and are prepared to face it. There comes a point when self-protection can be dangerous to those it is designed to protect. However, both of these points were lost on those too far removed to grasp them. This was especially true in Afghanistan where most of our time was spent walking over extremely rough terrain at high elevations; adding an extra seventy pounds of excess weight would make us ineffective as war fighters and, even worse, an easier target. I learned many valuable lessons working with the Special Forces (SF). One was "don't die angry," meaning that if I wear all of this armor and I die anyway, I'll die angry.

One of the key phrases of the Infantry is "Shoot, Move, Communicate," because these three things are essential for maximum impact against our enemy. Trying to shoot, move and communicate while carrying extra weight and sucking wind is difficult at best. This is another reason we wanted to work as far away from the "Flag Pole" as soon as possible. The ICTs would demand that we were in full uniform compliance regardless of the impact on us or the mission. Once again it was not about reality, only the paperwork. We left base in full battle array and dumped our armor as soon as we were on foot.

TAJIMEN

The most valuable assets we had during our time in Afghanistan were our interpreters, known as Tajimen (Talking men) by the ANA. Well beyond just translating information, a good interpreter could translate cultural meaning as well. We had two groups of interpreters: those who had left Afghanistan when they were young and had been educated in either America or the United Kingdom (UK), and those who had been raised only in Afghanistan. The first group learned English and their native language (Dari or Pashtu) immersed in western culture. They understood the slang and other cultural nuances of the English language, whereas the second group learned English in class from a teacher with very little cultural relevance. They could translate words but not their cultural meaning.

It was imperative to know your interpreter and his background because it would determine how in-depth your discussion was in regards to translation. An interpreter with limited cultural background could completely misrepresent your point without meaning to, while a good interpreter could not only explain your point succinctly but could also explain the Afghan meaning to you as well. One "local" interpreter translated a question I had in regards to the number of vehicles in our convoy. He responded with an answer about the weather. That was innocent enough and easy to address. A bad example of this occurred between me and an interpreter I will name "Forked Tongue." He became my new Interpreter when my previous had been scooped up by the SF—he was that good. While time passed I began to sense that my relationship with my Afghan counterpart CPT A-top had begun to suffer and I did not know why.

I began to suspect my interpreter was not translating well and I asked another interpreter I trusted to listen in on our conversations. Sure enough Forked Tongue was indeed translating poorly, but what was worse, he was doing it purposely. He was playing me against A-top for his own benefit. When I could confirm this I confronted him with my suspicions and he was indignant that I would make such a claim. Understanding the culture, I did not make this claim in front of other Afghan men, otherwise he would be honor bound to kill me. Regardless of his denial, I was confident that he had lied to me and A-top and I dismissed him as my interpreter. Due to the nature of our relationship of trust with our interpreters, he was fired.

A short time later I was informed that FT had placed a bounty on me and swore to kill me himself when I traveled outside of YD. When I spoke with A-top about this threat he was furious for two reasons: not only had FT disrespected him by lying, he also disrespected A-top by threatening me, as I was under A-top's protection. I asked A-top how we should handle this, and he stated that we were honor bound to go find FT and kill him.

By this time I was still conflicted in my spirit about killing, not that killing my enemies was wrong, but how I felt about it was eating at me. I had already shot and killed enemy soldiers in both Iraq and Afghanistan, but that was while they were shooting at me. Actually going to FT's home with the intention of executing him for a threat was somewhere I had not gone before. Additionally, I would have to leave YD without permission, and if I was killed, captured or arrested I would be in serious trouble and would get little support from my own command.

I discussed this with A-top and he understood that I was coming from an entirely different military culture and he stated that he would take care of it. I learned a few days later that A-top and his staff found FT and beat him in front of his family. FT broke and begged for his life; that act demonstrated that he was a coward which was a worse death in Afghanistan than actually dying. A-top left him alive, warned and shamed; I had nothing to fear from FT ever again.

BATHROOM HUMOR

To say that there are cultural differences between Americans and those from the Middle East is an understatement. What I will share is not meant to demean any particular ethnic group or religion, but rather to find some humor in our differences in the hope that we can laugh at ourselves. During my first tour in Iraq there was an issue with Iraqi workers on our base using the Porta Johns (PJ). It is customary for Arabs to wipe themselves using only their hand. They also do not use American toilets. Rather they squat over a hole in the floor or outside on the ground.

This came to a head (head is a military term for bathroom) when it was discovered that the Iraqis were using the PJs in conjunction with their cultural norms. They did not sit on the seat but rather they squatted over it leaving excrement everywhere. They also refused to use toilet paper, claiming it would violate their religious traditions to do so. Before long, most of the PJs were a mess. Therefore the base sanitation contractor segregated a few of them for Iraqi use only. Written in Arabic over the door was "Iraqi," and inside these units the seat and toilet paper were removed and in its place were a bottle of water and an outline of feet drawn on either side of the hole. The solution worked like a charm.

Afghans, like Iraqis, are Muslim, but that is where most of the similarities end. Afghans will use a smooth stone instead of their hand (or toilet paper); obviously paper is rare in countries with so few trees. Most Afghans that used the PJs seemed to have better aim then their Iraqi cousins but the trouble started when trucks came in to service the PJs. These trucks run a hose down into the tank that holds all of the waste and then, with a powerful pump, suck the waste up into a tank. It seems that the Afghans were using stones to clean themselves and then depositing them into the PJ tank. When the pump engaged it sucked all those stones up the hose and into the motor trashing it. It sounded like someone had dumped a load of rocks into a wood chipper.

Being one of the ETTs it fell upon me to handle the situation, which I did as tactfully and quickly as possible. I held a class on how to use the PJ correctly to include sitting on the seat and using toilet paper in place of a stone. The Afghan soldiers were actually thrilled with the idea of not using stones anymore and using paper instead; it's the little things that matter.

Later in my Afghan tour while based at a remote site I built a PJ of my own designed on a scene I saw in the movie *Platoon* (Stone, 1986) where Charlie Sheen's character had latrine duty. I built a wooden box that sat inside an old Soviet conex. Inside the box was a metal barrel cut in half that I could pull out periodically for cleaning, this is the part that the Afghans could not understand. After removing the barrel from the box I would pour some diesel fuel into it, stir it (hence the term Poop Soup) and light it. It burns rather well thus destroying the disease ridden pile. No matter how I tried to explain the benefits of this process, the Afghan soldiers could not get past the fact that I was burning good fuel. This was just another example of cultural barriers that were difficult to cross when that was even possible, and sometimes it gave us something to chuckle about.

CHAPTER FIFTEEN

MY DANCES WITH WOLVES TOUR: FORT APACHE

Upon finally arriving at our new base, it was obvious that this place was by definition a Forward Operating Base. There was nothing beyond this base other than a few Outposts strategically located on the top of the mountains surrounding this place. This base was no larger than YD with even fewer amenities, and it was located near a small town in a remote province near the Pak border. While I was coming to grips with the realization that this mission would be rather basic in its available comforts, I had no idea that our orders had already been amended.

This frontier post, that I'll call Ft. Apache, had no PX, cold showers on odd days and a chow hall that was a step up from eating MREs. By the time it had taken us to convoy here I was looking forward to being away from the flagpole. CPT Casey and I had developed a bond with each other and a great working relationship with our ANA. I could deal with the lack of comforts a larger base would provide if the rest of my tour was on these terms.

The United States soldiers that we were there to help greeted us warmly. It seemed that the enemy had complete control between a major river and the border. It was all our guys could do to defend the post and work their side of the river; the enemy was exploiting the fact that there was only one bridge crossing that river for a hundred miles in either direction. Our forces could not deal with that threat without first crossing that bridge which could be seen for miles. No surprise meant that the enemy could either withdraw further up the mountains or have ample time to set up an ambush.

I will not forget the look on their faces when I stated that we would do what we could, but I did not see how much help we would be in only two weeks. Their faces froze for second and asked me to repeat myself, after which they stated that their understanding was that we were there to stay long-term. CPT Casey responded with the next obvious question which was "Even if that is true, we will still have to cross that same bridge, so we're no better off than you are." It was at that time we received our amended orders and discovered that we were to cross that bridge and build a FOB from the ground up.

"With what materials and equipment?" CPT Casey asked.

"Our assets are five United States soldiers, one hundred and fifty ANA, and a dozen trucks."

We were advised that we would have the support we needed. There was heavy equipment at Apache that we could access and we were actually taking over an abandoned Taliban base, so how bad could it be?

Further investigation revealed why our orders had been changed. Another active duty unit was originally assigned this border mission, but those in command of that unit decided that they did not want any part of it and were persuasive in having our orders amended. We were not pleased with the situation, yet I would come to realize that if God had not orchestrated this change Himself, He certainly put it to good use. I knew that He was with me no matter where I was in the world, and that He was always willing and able to repair my broken spirit.

FOB GILLIGAN

We notified our CoC back at YD about our "amended" orders before agreeing to the new mission. Our CoC advised us to make the best out of this new mission until they could investigate it further. We left Ft. Apache and convoyed toward FOB Gilligan, a name I gave it due to our ever-changing orders that seemed to keep us marooned in the frontier. When we approached the bridge I could see the issue immediately. Not only was it impossible to cross this bridge without being seen for miles around, but it was little more than a one lane bridge, a natural choke point. I mentioned my concern about being so openly vulnerable on the bridge to A-Top. He stated that the enemy would not attack us on the bridge for fear of destroying the only way across this river; they would wait until we are across.

Once across, we had to dismount and walk the next five miles due to the poor condition of the road. A continuous series of potholes and ruts made it impossible to drive faster than walking. We stopped at a small village and asked the elders why the road was in such poor condition. They stated that it used to be better and that traffic used to pass through this village on the way to the Pakistan border, but the Taliban had ruined the road in order to slow the American and ANA soldiers, making them easier targets. We learned that just past our new FOB was a mountain pass that led into Pakistan, but because of the increased presence of the Taliban few people dared travel that route anymore. This decreased traffic was creating an economic hardship on the local Afghans. Improving the road and opening the pass would be one of the first projects we sought to undertake.

Eventually it seemed that our rocky trek was over as we approached our new FOB. It was not a base but rather a compound that looked more like a medieval castle. My first thoughts were that we could make this work; at least we would have a defensible base to start with as we made necessary improvements. Yet when we approached the building we were met with a dozen armed Afghan policemen on top of the wall and the Chief of Police at the gate with his own escort. A-Top immediately approached the Chief and engaged him with the customary cultural greetings as the ANA began to fan out around the building. There was no love lost between the ANA and the police, because many believed that the Afghan police were corrupt and were not to be trusted. I thought this was going to end badly when our Terp explained that the Provincial Governor had given the police custody of this building and we were to occupy a different base. I liked this base. It was close to the river and was surrounded by several hundred yards of open land which we could use as a "killing field" (that cleared area around a base that is designed for killing enemy attackers).

A-Top advised us that we needed to move on to the next location. The Provisional Governor was a known Taliban hack, but A-Top did not have the rank to go above him. In addition, trying to force the police out would most likely end in bloodshed. Having to submit to this level of corruption was difficult for my buddies and I, but we trusted A-Top's advice and moved on. I believe corruption is the most common denominator between third-world countries, based on my time overseas. But that is another book for another day.

Realizing that we weren't in Kansas anymore, our convoy of the homeless pushed forward. We stopped momentarily a few miles further to once again converse with the village elder who shared the real story behind our "new, new" base. It seems that when the Taliban heard that we were moving into that area they moved the police into our original building and we were to occupy a group of run down huts currently being used as stables for livestock. The enemy fully expected us to leave that area and abandon the mission to occupy the east side of the river. The Taliban could not imagine that we would occupy such an indefensible base.

Upon our arrival it was clear to all that we had been set up; this was not a base in anyone's country. There were no walls or even a defensible perimeter to speak of. Less than a dozen run down mud huts were present. Half of the buildings had little or no roof. Forget occupying the "high ground," these buildings were literally positioned at the base of the mountain range allowing the enemy to pummel us with rocket and gun fire from above. Without exaggerating, the enemy could throw rocks at us and do damage. Not to mention the basic amenities, no water, no electricity and of course no latrines.

We surveyed the situation and discussed our options with A-Top, ultimately deciding to stay. We all realized that the Taliban expected us to leave, but it is always good to be unpredictable in warfare. That was one of the key factors to the Soviet's defeat in Afghanistan in the 1980s. The Soviets would not change their SOPs and became amazingly predictable, and we would not follow their example. Another well taken point presented by A-Top was morale. We had traveled for days over mountains and through dangerous terrain with one thought in mind, find the enemy and kill him. To leave now would not only damage the morale of the ANA soldiers, but it would also lessen A-Top's standing with his men. As the Commander/Warlord, that was not acceptable.

The real work was just ahead of us, A-Top set up firing positions on the hill tops above us as well as along the base perimeter. I use the term perimeter loosely; there was no more than a line drawn around the buildings we occupied. Beyond the edge of our FOB were beautiful fields of the most colorful flowers that I had ever seen. I asked my interpreter what type they were. "Poppies," he replied, "for the Opium trade." The next question that came up from one of my fellow soldiers was, "are we going to leave it alone or burn it?" We discussed this issue over chai with A-Top. His advice was simple and direct, "We are not here to burn flowers; we are here to kill Taliban." A-Top proceeded to explain to us the reality of the Opium trade in Afghanistan. These larger fields are owned by warlords who would have us killed for destroying their investment. Additionally, these fields are worked on and maintained by the local farmers who have few opportunities to earn hard currency in the first place, and they would not dare to deny the warlord his invitation to work in his fields. We were in Afghanistan to kill the Taliban and win the hearts and minds of the local people. That would be difficult if we denied the villagers the only real source of income they had. I realize the terrible destruction that the opium/heroin trade has wreaked upon the world, yet that fight was not ours at this time.

There was one small mud hut with an intact roof that we Americans decided to live in while the ANA occupied the few remaining huts and set up tents. We immediately realized that it was not wise to place all of us in one building because one enemy rocket or grenade could take out our entire team. We decided to take turns sleeping in our truck since there were no more suitable buildings left. I volunteered to sleep there every night rather than rotate soldiers; it just seemed to make more sense.

CPT Fenton and SFC Moore at FOB Gilligan.

Ft. Apache did manage to give us what few materials they could spare, like Constantina Wire (C-wire), sandbags and shovels. The wire was strung-out around key areas in order to deny the enemy easy access onto the base. Fighting positions (similar to the foxholes of earlier wars) were re-enforced with sandbags along with a working gate. This was also the beginning of really getting to understand the Afghan/Muslim culture.

As an NCO in the American Army I immediately went to work filling sandbags on my own in order to build a re-enforced position for the American team. My interpreter came to me and asked me to stop working.

"You are causing us shame SSG Moore. You are an important guest so you cannot labor; it is not right."

He explained that in their culture important people never did manual labor, and by my actions I demonstrated that either I am not important or that my host is not looking after me. I responded with the fact that it needed to get done and that I did not see the ANA soldiers doing any labor to improve our defenses. He further explained that is because they are warriors and it is beneath them to do such work. Afghan men who engage in manual labor are lower on their caste system so the ANA refused to basic labor.

My frustration level was climbing for obvious reasons. Improving our defenses was not an option, so if the Taliban was going to hit us it would be at this time. It would take some effort on my part to get past the assumption that they were just rationalizing their laziness and begin to understand that we did come from different military cultures. It was imperative that we find a way around this impasse in such a way that everyone saved face and the job got done.

We met with the village elders and explained that we needed to hire some of the men for paid labor at our camp. They agreed to send a dozen men each morning, individually chosen by the elders, and paid by them after we paid the elders for providing the labor. Day after day they came to fill sandbags, string c-wire and improve buildings. By employing the locals we won their trust, infused their local economy with hard currency and our working relationship flourished.

Realizing that Afghanistan was littered with unexploded ordinance (bombs of different types), we advised the locals to bring what they found to us for disposal. This served several purposes. Every bomb we destroyed was one less used against us, and it possibly saved the life of another Afghan who may stumble onto it. The locals also became our eyes and ears in that area. They provided us with information about the enemy's movements, ambush plans, IED placements and other useful intelligence. While we were there we brought heavy equipment in to improve the roads, provided school supplies and dug wells for clean water. Granted, all of these improvements were paid for with American tax dollars, but these were permanent landmarks that these locals would see day after day with the knowledge that the American soldiers were here and the locals are better off for it. I cannot emphasize this last point enough. The fact that Afghans thought every United States soldier was a Christian meant that I never missed an opportunity to leave a positive lasting impression, not only for the glory of God, but to counter any negative experiences they may have had.

Another instance of cultural conflict arose at chow time. The United States military is designed in such a way that runs counter to most other countries, especially in regards to their military. Those of higher rank are treated best and take position over those beneath them in status. This was demonstrated at mealtime when the lowest private eats first because those with rank are responsible for their welfare, resulting in those with higher rank eating last. When the ANA had established a make-shift kitchen and announced that chow was ready, CPT Casey and I went to the back of the line. Declining to eat first created a commotion. Our interpreter explained again that it was unacceptable for us to not only eat last, but that we should not be getting our own food; others would bring our food to us. That was a difficult concept to accept for Casey and me. It was counter to everything we had been trained to do. A-Top then invited us to eat with him in his tent and ordered his men to serve us. This was the beginning of what I like to call my "Dances with Wolves" tour. Due to living off base and with the ANA, immersed in their culture, I began to relate to that movie even more as time passed.

A RUGGED AND BEAUTIFUL COUNTRY!

HOME IMPROVEMENT

Now that we had a consistent supply of labor and the immediate concern of base security was settled, I began to consider long-term plans for our team. Since our arrival at FOB Gilligan, most of our team had been living in a very small mud hut and I had been sleeping in a Ford Ranger. I discovered a larger building with a solid roof and asked why no one was living there. The Afghans stated that it had been used as a stable and was full of cow manure, which they could not touch as part of their religion.

CPT Casey had gone on a resupply mission, so I enlisted the help of another member of our team, SGT Red. Together he and I began the filthy work of shoveling that building out. Since the ANA wanted nothing to do with that building, working on it ourselves did not offend them. In fact, they thought we were "dewana," or crazy, for doing it at all. Two days of shoveling manure (and stacking sandbags to reinforce the walls) and the main room was empty. Before we could move in there were still other improvements to be done. The floor and walls were hardened mud, and we would have choked on the dust if we did not find coverings.

I convinced A-Top to go shopping with us at the local bazaar to buy furniture and other necessities, to which he readily agreed, knowing that I would also buy his favorite, lamb kabobs.

When Casey returned we had furnished the room with floor mats, wall hangings (to keep the dust from the mud walls to a minimum), and a few tables and lawn chairs. This building also had a covered porch that we equipped with a table and chairs for our meetings and morning coffee. Since we had doubled the width of the walls, we built a firing position for our 240 Bravo machine gun so our room could be used as a fighting position as well.

This work definitely made our time there more tolerable, but the cultural ramifications were interesting. One of the obvious needs we had was a latrine, and for the first two weeks the Americans were making do with the "Hadji Squat" (this term became synonymous with the way many in that part of the world squat rather than sit on the ground) over a hole in the ground. While at the bazaar I purchased an extra plastic chair, cut the center out and we now had a toilet seat of sorts. It's the little things that you notice when you do not have them.

A tense moment did arise when the ANA doctor saw what we had done to improve our living quarters. He liked what he saw and asked me who would live there (he spoke English). I explained that I would. He replied with "You SGT, I live here now," implying that his rank as an ANA officer trumped mine. After all the work that had gone into fixing up our new home I was not about to surrender it to anyone. More importantly, the fact that this particular Afghan was a worthless political appointment who received his medical degree from what I assume was the "Kabul school of medicine and VCR repair," I stood up to face him and replied.

"SGT Moore dig shit; SGT Moore live here!"

He stepped forward and began to raise his hand to strike me, which would have been the appropriate response in his culture for someone he saw as being from a lower class speaking in such a defiant manner. It was then that he noticed I had already drawn my knife and he froze. Staring straight into his eyes I told him that if he did not leave I would cut off his right hand and if he ever tried to hit me I would kill him. He was stunned and at a loss for what to do. No one had ever spoken to him in such a manner before. In conjunction with the fact that I already knew him to be a coward, he backed up and out of my room.

I related this to CPT Casey and the others; we decided to share it with A-Top who had no use for this doctor either but was stuck with him temporarily. This doctor was very typical of a country with a corrupt political system. He was appointed to this rank and position purely based on who his family was and not on any earned merit. He was a lowlife who took the free, basic medical supplies provided to him by the United States Army and either sold them to a drugstore in Kabul, or would require soldiers to pay him for treatment.

One day, while walking to another base, we were attacked in the middle of the village (an event I will elaborate on later). When it was over we discovered that this same doctor had been shot in the arm while running away from the fight; it was not fatal, but was enough to have him sent back to Kabul. Not a bad day after all.

THE GOOD SERGEANT

I wanted to maintain a balance between doing my duty (regardless of where it led) and not losing myself in the violence. I am reminded of a scene from *Saving Private Ryan* (Spielberg, 1998) when Tom Hank's character stated that whenever he killed an enemy soldier a part of him died, and he was afraid that when he got home there would not be enough of him left for his wife to recognize. I could not have stated it better myself. That was a legitimate fear of mine, what I would look like spiritually and emotionally when I got home if I did not get a handle on my hatred for our enemy.

Throughout my tour in Afghanistan, I made every effort to spend time in prayer and devotions, I did not like where I had gone spiritually with my thoughts toward Muslims. While living with the ANA at FOB Gilligan I took more notice of their prayer time, hard to miss considering they stopped everything five times per day to pray (or nap, depending on how serious they were about their faith). I like to begin and end my days with prayer so I decided to do so outside under the covered porch we had built.

One morning, while drinking coffee made from re-used coffee grounds and cocoa, I noticed an ANA soldier staring at me. We exchanged greetings and he asked me what I was reading. I responded, "Holy Book," to which he replied with a smile, "Good SGT!" His response gave me pause; I wondered what he actually thought about my Christian faith and my "Holy Book." I asked our interpreter what their thoughts were on my faith.

Their consensus was that most Afghans were nominal Muslims, meaning that they were following Islam because it is the religion of their fathers; it is intertwined with their cultural and national identity. Yet they also realize that they were given no choice in the matter, and probably found themselves just going through the motions. It is what's expected of them. This claim can also be made of many American Christians as well, however I do not know of one that threatens to kill you for deciding to leave the faith when you are an adult. This religion by threat of force can hardly endear someone to a relationship with a loving God; then again, Muslims do not believe that they can have a relationship with Allah the same way that Christians do with our Savior. Before leaving Afghanistan I would meet ANA soldiers who would tell me in confidence that they "wanted to go to America because there were no Muslims there!" Through further discussion, their meaning was clear. They wanted out of Islam and its forced adherence.

Back to the original question I asked of my interpreters. They believe that many of the Afghan soldiers saw my expression of faith as an indication that I was a righteous man. Being a man of faith carried much more weight with these soldiers than I was originally aware of, and it caused me to ponder, pray and read scripture all the more. I was then moved by the Spirit to look beyond myself and to realize that God had brought me out here in the Afghan wilderness to be a light for these Muslim soldiers, and that otherwise they would never be able to see.

It was always this way between God and me. Whenever I was self-absorbed with my own situation He would drop someone into my lap that obviously needed His love and I was the only vessel to carry it to them at that time. It reminds me that God knows my nature so much better than I do. He knows that when push comes to shove, I will always do whatever is necessary for whomever He places in my path. This process always leads me to a better place spiritually as well. I find it impossible to share what He has done for me without seeking His face once more.

From that moment forward I sought to live purposefully, as a Christian who wants to glorify God in such a way that even these Muslim soldiers and villagers would have to see it. I needed to balance my role as a soldier and as a Christian. Not that the two are mutually exclusive, but in their culture men are warriors or they are nothing. I sought to become the warrior they would follow and the man of faith they would respect. They would not respect my faith if they did not first respect me as a man. One thing I had always done but decided to make =more obvious was to pray just prior to going outside the wire on a dangerous mission.

Sure enough, some of the ANA saw what I was doing and asked the interpreter to inquire. I explained that I was praying that God would protect us during this mission and that when we found the enemy He would make us brave, fast and accurate. The ANA like this prayer because it reinforced their cultural perception as holy warriors and the reality, as one stated to me, "If we kill enough Taliban they will leave our country, then we can go home." From that point forward some of the soldiers would ask me to pray for them before we left for the mission. They wanted the Terp to tell them what I was "saying" so I decided to begin each prayer with one of my favorite verses, "Blessed be the Lord, my rock, who trains my hands for war, and my fingers for battle" (Psalm 144:1, NASB). I knew that they understood "the Lord" to mean Allah, but I thought it was a foundation from which to build on.

Making friends with a remote mountain tribe.

CHAPTER SIXTEEN

THE BORDER WAR

The remaining months that we spent at FOB Gilligan were filled with a regular routine of nighttime patrols, setting up ambushes, repairing the road, digging wells and dispensing school supplies. That seemed to sum up most of my entire tour, taking the fight to the enemy while trying to improve the life of the Afghan people, winning hearts and minds as they say.

Shortly after we established a presence at FOB Gilligan we were joined by a team of SF soldiers on horseback, not something you see every day. The Afghan terrain, being as rough as it is, forced the soldiers to make use of local Nuristan ponies (Nuristan is a province in north central Afghanistan known for its hardy mountain ponies). These ponies were necessary for moving equipment and men across the mountainous terrain. Working with the SF brought our fight to a whole new level; adaptability and force of action were the foundation of all our missions forward. Along with horses, they also brought assets that I would not have had available otherwise, such as satellite imagery, dedicated air support, upgraded weapons and (my favorite) ice cream. It may not sound like a big deal at home, but after a few months of eating goat and drinking old coffee, ice cream sandwiches are the bomb!

Our missions became more intense, more involved and far more dangerous, and I was all for it. The more we went out with the SF and began to engage the enemy at a whole new level the more I yearned for an opportunity to kill them. I could not forget the words of the ANA soldier who wanted to kill the enemy so he could finally go home and live with his family in peace, and I felt driven to make that happen. The more time I spent with the ANA the closer we became as friends and brothers in arms. The more tolerance I had for Muslims, the more I hated and wanted to kill the people who had perverted their religion for their own political gain.

I have to admit that if I was meant to be engaged in multiple direct combat actions I could not have planned it better. Here I was, just a National Guard NCO, working with Afghan Mujahedeen fighters and our own SF. I was living large. The biggest irritation I had with my first and last tours was the sense that we constantly hid from the enemy or ran away from them. I acknowledge the missions were different, yet being with these two groups together was more than I could have hoped for. It is not that I thirst for violence and death, but my attitude had always been that of an infantry soldier; my mission is to kill the enemy, not run and hide. I could not understand and didn't have much patience for those military personnel who came to a war zone acting as nothing more than a tourist collecting hazardous duty pay while having their picture taken on camels they will never actually ride. The focus of these groups was to go out to "pick a fight" to paraphrase William Wallace's character in *Brave Heart* (Gibson, 1995). The sole purpose of every mission was to find and kill the enemy regardless of where that took us or what hardships we may endure.

There were certain complications involved since our three groups had three different CoCs and therefore different parameters of what we could and could not do. One such example was the directives we were under in regards to the Pakistan border. The SF could go anywhere they needed to—even cross it, the ANA could not cross the border and my small group was not allowed within five kilometers (K) of the border. The restriction alone on my group should tell you everything you need to know about our CoC.

During one such mission I was with a team of SF and a platoon of ANA. Our mission was to follow a trail up the mountain range near the Pakistan border in search of a point where the Taliban would cross with weapons and explosives. After an entire day of climbing over a mountain range I double checked my GPS with my map, believing we had indeed crossed over the Pakistan border. I quietly approached the SF leader with my revelation that I thought we were "off the map." He asked, "Who can really say for certain where the border is?" Before I could respond, he stated that the mission dictated that we cross over. The enemy counts on us to not cross the border so they store their weapons over the other side prior to an attack. If we do not go and get them they will attack us with impunity much the way the Viet Cong used the Ho Chi Minh trail during the Viet Nam war. He assured me that I would not get into trouble with our CoC, if questioned my response was simply an honest one, I cannot say for a fact that I was ever inside of Pakistan. A few months later I was called to report to two officers that I did not know and when that one question was asked I replied honestly, "I cannot say for a fact that we were ever in Pakistan." Adding innocently, "I'm National Guard, what do I know!" This may not seem like a big deal to some, but it speaks volumes about those who were concerned with paperwork and regulations and the war fighters I was with who were concerned about winning the war by killing the enemy.

There were several missions similar to this one on the border. Some were more dangerous than others; some were no longer than a day while others lasted for several days. One in particular was a major offensive designed to surround the enemy. The Taliban had adapted to our border crossings and had actually moved their bases inside the Afghan border. It appeared that they were planning an offensive of their own with the intent of over running our base. The internet we received stated that the Taliban not only wanted to push us back across the river, but wanted to try and take soldiers prisoners for PR purposes. The SF had attained a copy of the Taliban's directive on how to torture Americans. I will not get into the details, but it makes "water boarding" look like child's play. I loved working with the SF and the Mujahedeen ANA because their attitude was that if it is a fight the enemy wants then we will see that they have it.

Our intelligence revealed that they were gathering forces in a mountain valley not far above FOB Gilligan. Our plan was to fly several platoons of combined forces in Chinook helicopters above their positions. This would give us the high ground and cut off their escape back to Pakistan while our remaining forces would start a ground offensive pushing them toward us. This story is relevant not because of the mission itself but what I learned about myself and the ANA.

Prior to most of our dangerous missions the average Afghan soldier was not informed about it due to OPSEC. Occasionally, we would discover a Taliban operative working in the ANA. Obviously the last thing we wanted was to attempt a mission only to discover the enemy was waiting for us. This being said when we trucked the ANA soldiers to the landing zone (LZ) my interpreter informed me that none of the ANA had ever flown before. Most of these men were simple tribal herders who had lived without electricity most of their lives. Through my interpreter I explained to them what our mission was and how we were going to enter and exit the Chinook. I told them to keep their eyes on me at all times and we would get through this part of the mission okay. I was impressed that though they were obviously anxious about flying they were excited to go. I later learned that my interpreter added that they were specifically chosen because of their courage and that it would bestow honor upon their families, there was no turning them back.

We boarded the Chinook without any drama but exiting was entirely different. Due to the sudden turn of bad weather, we could not be dropped at the designated LZ. To make matters worse, the Crew Chief informed us that we would not be able to land and that we would need to "jump off" the back of the Chinook onto the side of a cliff. Before that could sink in we were there and the U.S. troops on board with us were jumping. I told the ANA to watch the others exit and to do the same, following me. It was hard to determine the height we were jumping at but the worst part was the Chinook bouncing up and down while we were trying to exit.

All members of our party landed safely but when the crew pushed our supplies off the Chinook they missed the cliff and all of our water went crashing down the side of the mountain along with half of our food. We secured the LZ and contacted the air base about our lost supplies. They informed us that they would not return for resupply due to the weather. I half-believed the weather excuse and thought more about the vulnerability of a Chinook hovering so close to the side of a mountain. Chinooks are a very big target when they are hovering and a big prize for the Taliban, something we all have seen too many news reports about.

We were dropped at what is known as a hot LZ (a landing zone that is either currently under fire or at risk of being), and we needed to move to our designated rally point and establish a defensive position before the enemy realized what was happening. Some of the ANA volunteered to climb down the cliff after our lost supplies; I was advised that to refuse their request to go would dishonor them regardless of the inherent danger. While climbing up over the cliff I had difficulty due to the thin air at that elevation and that I was carrying extra provisions. I always prided myself as an infantryman who could travel light. There is a saying, "Carry what you need but need what you carry." Yet when packing for this mission I had a strong urge to take an extra pack of water. It seems my guardian angel was looking out for me again—that extra water would make all the difference.

Regardless of the strain I pushed on, not wanting the ANA to see me struggle. Yet I came upon a cliff that I could not manage with both packs and my weapon. While I attempted the climb an ANA soldier reached down and asked to carry my extra pack, not wanting to look weak I declined. He stuck out his hand again and said "Friend." My interpreter then explained that he wanted to help me because I was his friend, not because I was weak. I did not know this particular Afghan soldier very well, but I had definitely made an impact upon him somehow. I later learned that he had been watching me, how I pray before mission and read my Holy Book, and he believed that I was a friend of the Afghans. Once again the Lord had placed me in a situation where I was not only dependent upon a Muslim for help, but that by submitting to the Spirit's leading I had made an impact on some of these Muslim soldiers. I was then conflicted in a different way. I was thrilled that I was glorifying God with my testimony, and yet filled with self-loathing at the thought of the darkness my heart still held.

Upon reaching our destination, we set up a perimeter along the ridge line near the Pakistan border overlooking the valley below. Two other groups had been dropped onto ridgelines on either side of ours. We now had control of the high ground and all access to the border. Realizing the weather was only getting worse, the captain and I looked for shelter for our extended stay. We found the remains of a shallow cave and used ponchos to cover the entrance and moved our gear inside. The rest of our time up there was filled with torrential downpours every night, making sleep almost impossible and causing the temps to drop even more. Yet I would not have wanted to be anywhere else. Here we were away from the Flag Pole and the ridiculous regulations of the ICTs. Here I believed I was relevant to our mission and the war. Here I would matter!

OUR TEMPORARY HOME DURING THE BORDER MISSIONS.

A small amount of our water was recovered but not enough to sustain the number of personnel that we had, especially with the physical exertion that they had to endure. We assigned a team of ANA that were familiar with the area to scout out sources of water while we pushed on with the mission. It was not long before we were becoming an ineffective unit due to the lack of water. The captain and I discussed sharing what water we had with the ANA and decided it would be the best course of action. I spoke with the ANA NCO and gave him most of the water we had left; he was so grateful that I almost became embarrassed by his carrying on.

This had a significant impact on this group of ANA. The fact that I shared my water with them elevated me to an entirely new level. Later one of the soldiers asked why I gave them my water and I replied that God would want me to share with my brothers. I stated that we are all brothers in His eyes, created by Him to glorify Him. The ANA soldier replied that Allah is great, SGT Moore is good. I share this again for the impacts we can have with such small gestures of kindness to those who would least expect it.

A few days later, we were informed that a group of armed Taliban was making a break for the border. With a squad of ANA and SF we ran to cut them off and hopefully engage them. We arrived at the border where the only defining line was a rusty old barbed wire fence that a cow could push over. I was walking toward the fence when all at once a dozen Pakistan soldiers jumped up from the scrub brush with their AKs pointed at me shouting "get down." I froze in place and pushed my selector switch from safe to semi but did not raise my rifle, nor was I about to lay down for anyone.

The ANA were in front of me in an instant, including Abraham, shouting back at the Pakistani soldiers with their rifles raised and ready. I realized that this situation was about to go terminal if these soldiers did not cool down. My interpreter explained that the Pakistani soldiers were warning the ANA that they could not come within fifty meters of the border or they would shoot them. The ANA told them that they were Afghan soldiers and that they would walk where they pleased while inside their own country.

The SF and I approached the Pakistani soldiers with our interpreters and asked to speak with their commander while we convinced the ANA to lower their weapons. The ANA hesitated but when I stood in front of them and pointed my rifle down toward the ground they did the same. Once the Pakistani soldiers saw this they lowered their weapons as well. The SF soldier with me stated quietly, "Well done, I thought we were about to be killed in the middle an international incident."

I advised the ANA to withdraw most of their men into the scrub line so we would not pose such an aggressive posture. It would also give them some cover if things did go wrong. The Pakistan commander did arrive shortly and asked what we were doing there, I replied that we were looking for Taliban but we did not intend to cross the border into Pakistan. I continued with questions while they offered us chai. The most important question I asked was answered with a lie.

I pointed to a portion of the fence that had been tied back so passing under it was easy. There was also an obvious trail passing under this fence that continued off in both directions. I asked the Pakistani commander how many Taliban pass through the fence every week, to which he replied, "No Taliban here, no Taliban cross border." I asked the question again in a different manner but the answer was always the same, "No Taliban cross border." My interpreter then said to me quietly, "SGT Moore I think he is lying." I wanted to respond with "You think so!" But I knew he was being serious so I asked for his recommendation as to my next move. He stated, "If you call him a liar in front of his men he will probably shoot you. We can refuse his offer of hospitality (in regards to drinking the Chai offered) which will be insult enough, and then tell him that we will patrol wherever we wish without his permission, and speak like an Afghan man."

I understood what my interpreter meant. When an Afghan man speaks he never asks for permission or apologizes for anything, he just gives commands. I spoke like I was ready to jump over that fence and kill every soldier there; the Pakistani commander stated that he would contact his command. I turned and began walking away while he was still speaking to me. Turning your back on a man in that culture was another insult. We quickly moved out of sight and into cover to watch their reaction. The commander spoke with his men who were obviously angry, but made no move to cross the fence. He posted some of his soldiers at the fence and disappeared behind the guard shack. This interaction with the Pakistanis was tense, but it also elevated my standing with the ANA.

During our interaction with the Pak border patrol the enemy was making its way toward our position but was not looking for a fight because they were going to attempt to flank us and cross the border at another point. Yet with our forces pushing up from the valley and our other groups already in control of the border crossings along that ridge, their escape was doomed and they surrendered without incident. Most of the Taliban were conscripted goat herders who would have preferred to stay at home rather than get involved with this fight. The Taliban had a bad habit of forcibly taking young men from their homes under threat of death to a family member.

Later that evening I asked my interpreter why he knew that my aggressive approach would work. He stated, "I did not but I knew that if we backed down you would lose face with the ANA which would end your mission here. It would be better to die a man than to live as a coward. Now the ANA here will speak to the others of your courage today. Besides, I hate being lied too." We laughed at his last statement, but deep inside I wondered, "Who have I become?" And "Who will I be when I return home?"

That mission ended as they all do. However, returning to Fort Apache meant being flown back in the Chinooks. This meant having to jump onto the ramp of the Chinook while it hovered next to an outcropping of rocks overlooking another cliff. This was yet another adventure that ended as crazy as it started. We spent a few days at Fort Apache prior to returning to our FOB to shower and eat hot food.

I was approached by an SF member who I knew to be a Christian who stated that he had heard about the border incident. He asked if I was afraid during the exchange of challenges and insults. I honestly confessed that I was not at that moment, because I was angry and hate-filled. I shared more of my story with him, where I had come from and what my original motivation was for being there, and how I had learned that in dangerous situations anger and hatred gave me strength to face most anything.

His face became stoic and his eyes seemed distant for a moment, then he looked at me and stated that as a Christian he understood. That because of the atrocities that he had seen the enemy commit against civilians, especially women and children, it had become very easy to hate these people and even easier to kill them. He stated that it was a difficult balance to keep as a soldier and a Christian especially when faced with such obvious evil. I asked how he reconciled his actions and feelings with God.

I confessed to him that I was burdened, not by the fact that I had killed people, but that the more often it happened the easier it became and the less it bothered me. He stated that he believed that God approves of what soldiers have to do against evil men. He ended our discussion with this: "I intentionally seek God's face, I believe that in His presence my demons are diminished and those that are set against me are defeated, in His presence am I made whole again." He repeated, "Whole again but not unscarred, not without wounds that are reopened at a passing thought or worse, a nightmare. Actions have consequences, and that is the reality of the fallen world we live in, but praise God for His grace that we are able to pass through it."

CHAPTER SEVENTEEN

NIGHT RAIDS

The remainder of our time at FOB Gilligan seemed like a constant cycle of night missions, daily patrols, drinking chai with village elders and hanging out with the ANA. Our night missions were well orchestrated ambushes that the ANA and our teams would coordinate based upon intelligence we had received from the local villagers. It was not uncommon for the day workers to pass information about the movements of the Taliban to include the location of IEDs.

It was obviously unsettling when local village boys would arrive at our base with an unexploded mortar in their hand that they dug up. It was at that moment that we devised a new plan for the collection of bombs by the locals so that they would deposit them in a pit at the edge of our base where we could destroy them at a safe distance. We were amazed at first by the nonchalant attitude they had when handling explosives, yet it made sense when we considered the history of this country. These people have known nothing but war for more than a generation, handling explosives by children was just part of everyday life, and if they were injured or killed then it was "Allah's will."

During our down time I would hang out with the ANA. They especially enjoyed playing cards. The game we played seemed to be a cross between Hearts and Spades. Because of the language barrier I never got a good handle on it, but as long as money was not involved I was good. The funniest game I got pulled into playing was with three other Afghan soldiers all from different ethnic groups who could not speak more than their own language. They would not take no for an answer so I thought I would give it a try. By the end of the game I think I won two hands but lost the game and I still do not know how.

During the heat of the day we would sit under a tree or on my covered porch and talk about everything from politics, to marriage/ families, herding goats and even religion. It was during one of these bull sessions that one Afghan soldier that I was friends with asked why I would leave America to fight in Afghanistan? His question was based on two preconceived thoughts: One, why would anyone actually leave America? And two, if they did leave, why would any-one come to Afghanistan? Through my Terp I shared with them my original reasons for volunteering for my first tour to Iraq and why I volunteered again for Afghanistan. When I talked about my oldest son being in the Twin Towers in New York City I shared how angry I was because I thought he could have been killed. I did not realize it then but the translation they understood was that my oldest son had been killed by Al Qaeda and therefore I was in Afghanistan to avenge his death and restore my family's honor.

Living with the Afghans taught me many things about their cul-ture and about the Muslim faith in general. One of these was that was at the core of their familial relations was the oldest son. He is the "promised son" the one who bears his father's name and who will inherit the lion's share of his father's possessions. Learning the importance of the eldest son also explained why Mohammed and Muslim's today reject Isaac as Abraham's promised son. Ishmael was Abraham's first born son and therefore entitled to his father's blessing and inheritance (cf. Gen. 16:15-16; 21:2). It is through Ishmael that all of God's or Allah's promises would be fulfilled. This is such a foundational issue for them that they cannot get past it, which then leads them to believe that the Jews have lied about this event, making them heretics.

Knowing the background of the importance of the eldest son will explain why they began to treat me more as a brother than previ-ously. We had already become friends and they were so distraught at the thought of my oldest son being killed that they were determined to find a way to restore my family honor. I was surprised when my interpreter came to me late one night and stated that I must go with him. I was not suspicious of him because I had already trusted him with my life since we had arrived.

I got dressed and we walked to the back of the FOB to meet A-Top and a handful of ANA. It was not unusual for all of us to go out on night missions or for the ANA to go without us on their own. A-Top would tell us that they were going out without us because they were going to "fight the Afghan way." That meant that they would be going after an enemy and they were not going to follow any American ROEs.

A-Top told me that they had intelligence that a Taliban spy was nearby and they were going to "talk to him." The ANA version of "talking" usually began with intense intimidation; no one from this part of the world doubts the ANA's sincerity when it comes to extracting information. If the subject refused to talk they would begin with forced sodomy. That act alone usually ends with the ANA getting whatever intelligence they need, but if not, it is followed by physical torture and maiming, more sodomy and finally a dishonorable death.

Though I had grown to admire their hardworking character and sense of honor, the ANA's approach to certain things, like "talking" with the enemy, made it easier for me to dehumanize Muslims in general. Living with them was a process of two steps forward in friendship and then one step back.

I advised A-Top that I could not go with them if they were going to deal with an enemy spy in their traditional way. My interpreter explained to me how the translation of my son's story had been taken and they wanted to help me regain my family's honor. I looked around and saw a half dozen of my closest ANA friends looking at me with sad eyes, sad for my loss and with faces that were worn by the tragedies of their own losses. This was not just about me, they were going to regain their honor as well, and this was part of their journey too. My interpreter explained that for me to refuse this invitation would insult them and lessen my standing with them; there was no going back now.

We headed out of the FOB quietly but this time I was going without any other American soldiers. I was momentarily sick in my stomach, not for fear of what might happen outside the wire, but what would happen to me when I returned. Technically this was not the first time one of us had gone out with the ANA without other

United States soldiers, but it was the first time that no other member of my team knew about it. We moved along a trail that led toward the river and eventually into a small village. There my interpreter informed me that the ANA had already caught and restrained the Taliban spy and were holding him off FOB so he could be interrogated apart from the United States ROEs.

We were met by two ANA soldiers that I recognized as we were led into the compound. The compound belonged to an older Afghan that I immediately knew to be the village elder. It seems that he too had honor to reclaim since the Taliban would take the local girls as wives and sell them to the Arab Al Qaeda terrorists. The Arabs would "marry" them for the time they were in country and divorce them prior to leaving, which would cause the girls and their family's shame. Some girls were taken to their Arab "husbands" homes on the Arabian Peninsula to serve as unpaid domestic servants and sex slaves. This is yet another example of two steps forward and one step back for me and provided real context for why the Afghans despised all Arabs as much as they did.

The spy was dragged out to the courtyard and was dropped onto his knees in front of me. I noticed that they had tied his wrists to his ankles which served several purposes. It was impossible to run away in that position, it was uncomfortable for long periods and it made the threat of sodomy all the more real. He was a middle-aged Pashtu man dressed typically for that area. Yet there was something different about him, something sinister, more criminal than religious zealot. In my time as a police officer I had learned to read people by their eyes. I could read his well enough, this was not an Islamic warrior fighting to defend the faith. This was an opportunistic dirt bag playing for whichever team paid more and was most likely to win. I had met his kind before; he was a back shooter and a coward.

He appeared to be frightened until he saw my face and realized that I was an American. That must have calmed his fears somewhat, thinking that the ANA were going to turn him over to my custody. He also believed, and rightly so, that the Americans would not torture him and he would be taken to Bagram Air Base for questioning. I suddenly found myself in a position for which I was utterly unprepared. What did the ANA expect me to do with him and what was I willing to do to him? A-Top gave a command and three of the ANA moved to hold the spy down. "STOP!" I yelled at the ANA, which they did and looked at A-Top for direction.

My interpreter told me that if I did not do this thing the spy would not take me seriously; the enemy thinks that Americans are weak and cowardly. I told them that I did not need to rape a man to prove my manhood or my courage. I removed my 9mm pistol from its holster and walked over to the spy who smiled at me until he saw the pistol in my hand. Something that I had learned while in Iraq was that in most Muslim countries a pistol is the tool of execution. I had a hunch that he spoke enough English to understand me, so I asked who pays him and where is their compound. He refused and began to insult my mother; I shoved the barrel of my 9mm into his forehead and yelled my direction again. The ANA all took a few steps backwards away from the two of us; no one likes brain matter and blood splattered all over their clothes. I cocked the hammer all the way back and told him that I would count to three and pull the trigger. I counted to three, and then my pistol made a loud CLICK sound (I knew that I did not have a round in the chamber).

He broke and started to beg for mercy. I leaned forward and said, "you can talk to me now and I will send you to Bagram, or I will leave you with them. When they are done I will come back and I will shoot you myself, you have three seconds to decide. Three, two..." and then he cried out, "I talk."

I holstered my 9mm and turned to see all of my ANA brothers looking at me like I had just slain a dragon. I explained to A-Top that after they got what intelligence they needed from him (without harming him) they should bring him to our FOB the morning after I returned. That way A-Top could get all of the credit for bringing him in and there would be no questions asked about my participation.

The walk back to our FOB was somewhat surreal; I was not certain how to handle it or where it would take me. I decided to sit out on my make shift porch for a few moments to collect my thoughts before trying to sleep. It was then that I noticed my hands shaking uncontrollably. My muscles were twitching so fast that I had to put my cup of chai down. I was reminded of the scene in the movie *Saving Private Ryan* (Spielberg, 1998) where Tom Hanks character had the same type of shakes in his hands. My stomach sank as I realized that I had been lucky that night. What if the spy called my bluff? Would I have executed him or walked away? Walking away would have made working with the ANA impossible. They would have had no respect for me after that and what respect would I have for myself?

I came here to kill the enemy of my country and my family. What would I become if I walked away from that? What would I become if I had pulled the trigger?

The morning came earlier than I would have liked, but it was satisfying nonetheless. One of our interpreters came to our hut and advised us that the ANA had captured a Taliban spy and wanted the American soldiers to send him to Bagram. I purposely stayed away from exposing myself to the spy again in front of my team. Our team contacted our CoC and we were advised to transport him to a closer FOB than Bagram so that he could be interrogated there. We later learned that after being "lightly" questioned he was not sent to Bagram but was actually released!

A-Top was furious when he heard and stated that he would never turn over a prisoner to the Americans again. In his context he could not understand why we would let a known enemy go free, "If you know he is your enemy then you kill him, otherwise he will kill you." His logic made sense to me and it was times like these that I found myself conflicted by the actions of my own CoC. That has always been my issue with "Big Army." It is driven far too often by the PC agenda of whatever administration is in charge and loses touch with why we are fighting in the first place.

THE TOURISTS AMONG US

I share this story with the hope that it demonstrates how aggravating and possibly dangerous some situations may seem at times, only so that we may laugh at them later. I made it clear to those I was serving with that I was not a tourist and had little time for those in uniform who were. A typical Army tourist was a career desk jockey who volunteered for Afghanistan because at that time it was considered safer than Iraq. They arrive looking for the best rooms and chow halls and internet service. They have their pictures sitting on top of camels as if they were ever going to actually ride one. They are eager to get combat patches and ribbons but do not want to spend one night sleeping outside the wire on the ground.

That was fine as long as they remained close to the Flag Pole and left me and my men alone. Yet inevitably once we secured an area from a serious threat they would fly in for a few days of "combat duty." Waiting until the long hard road of the mission was done and show up at the end in order to add this mission to the list of their accomplishments. We would then waste time escorting them on short missions while they were hoping that someone would fire a couple of shots over our heads. That was their ultimate reason for being there anyway, to file paperwork for a CAB and leave.

One such group arrived explaining that they were there to "help" us with our mission. Great, I did not have time to be a tour guide. These officers were instructed to follow my direction on that evening's mission. Though they all outranked CPT Casey and me, we had been working that area for some time and knew best how to prepare for it. We explained that night's mission especially in regards to gear. The trek to the site was far and difficult and wearing too much gear would be tiring and noisy. After all, this was an ambush.

That evening came and a few of our guests arrived in full battle gear wearing every piece of equipment the Army could have possibly issued. Regardless of the reason, our recommendations were not heeded. Frustrated, I spoke with CPT Casey and he suggested using "controlled failure" as a teaching tool. That is a term used when you allow someone to screw up to the point they learn from it, but don't get hurt.

We moved out on foot breaking into three teams, one on each ridgeline overlooking the valley. Our team would secure a position behind a stone wall in the valley near the trail the enemy had used for night movement. My Terp shared with me that A-Top was concerned, he did not like taking these soldiers out, he thought they would get us killed. Yet he knew that orders were orders and we had no choice.

We walked for a few hours and settled into our position. This was an ambush which means sitting silently, any noise we make would be heard across the valley and give away our position. The two guests with me were offended when A-Top told them to "Shut Up," he knew that much English. They stopped talking and the night rolled forward slowly and quietly. One guest asked me why we were waiting so long and I quickly responded with a deer hunting analogy. "You don't walk into the woods five minutes before you expect the deer to arrive, you will lose the element of surprise." There could not be anything strange or out of place or the enemy would know it and either retreat or take us by surprise.

I was sitting there staring across the valley listening for any sounds and scanning the moonlit skyline for any movement when it happened. A sudden bright white light flashed all around us. I was immediately blinded and hit the ground face down. I was certain that the enemy had spotted us and had shot out a flare to expose our position. I waited for the sound of gunfire to begin and desperately hoped that my night vision would return so I could return fire.

When I could see I looked up to see A-Top crouched down like a cat about to pounce leaning toward one of our "tourists." I realized then that we were not under attack; one of our tourists was holding his camera with a dumbfounded look on his face. I asked him, "Sir, did you just take a picture?" To which he replied, "Yes, I wanted to take a picture of the river, was that bad?"

A-Top was now only a few feet away from him and all I could think was, "A-Top will kill him and I will have to bury the body!" A-Top froze for a moment looked at me and said, "Mission Bas (finished)!" My Terp stated that we were to head back to the base, the mission was over. While walking back I explained to the tourist why that was such a bad idea but that I would not mention it to the others in his group, I did not want to embarrass him. When I returned and briefed my commander I overheard the tourist telling the others what he had done and laughing about it. I wished A-Top had strangled him! He just did not get it. The leaders of the other two teams came to me and asked what had happened. One stated that, "The entire valley lit up, we could see all of you like it was daytime." Unfortunately this scenario would be repeated on too many occasions throughout my tour. Such is the burden of working with tourists and civilians in uniform.

Chapter Eighteen

Back to Yellow Dog

I never returned to FOB Gilligan, but I have seen pictures of it online since it has become a "real" FOB occupied by Big Army with walls, a chow hall and electricity. There was never a lack of missions, adventures and aggravations at FOB Gilligan, but I miss those days the most. Even though our living conditions were Spartan at best, we were masters of all that we surveyed. We answered to and depended on no one but our own team. We grew beards and wore the gear that we needed to wear, not what some distant ICT decided we must wear. We lived with the Afghans as they lived, and ate goat and fresh food every day. We talked about family, friends and the hope of better days to come. We were exhausted from night missions and daily patrols, yet even now I would go back if I could. Maybe it was the sense of being able to address any problem head on as creatively as we needed and the realization that we mattered at least on that small piece of Afghan rock.

Once we accomplished our mission, our orders changed and we traveled back to Yellow Dog for some badly needed equipment maintenance and showers. Although easier access to the internet was a welcomed change, the chow hall food was not. After eating the fresh unprocessed Afghan food my system did not appreciate the greasy Army food. We stayed at YD for a time working with the ANA on basic infantry tactics and logistics.

Another SF team arrived with specific orders to work directly with our ANA Company. It seems that Afghan President Karzai wanted to put an Afghan "face" on American missions, especially those executed by our SF units. Since we had already developed a working relationship with the ANA the decision was made to attach myself and some of the other embedded advisors to this SF group directly.

It would not be long before we were outside the wire again to "pick a fight." I thoroughly embraced that mindset, as a warrior it was my intent to seek out the enemy and kill them, if this was not our mission then send us home. Compared to my time traveling across Iraq in convoys hoping that we did not get shot at, our mission now was just the opposite. If the enemy shoots at us we know where he is.

Throughout the rest of my tour we went on "long walks" several times with the SF and ANA. Some missions were more successful than others depending upon the weather, terrain, Muslim holy days and interference from our own CoC. Another benefit of being attached to the SF meant that they could pull rank on our CoC and save us from being stuck on the base just to become typists. I was always amazed by the liberty the SF had to work as they needed too with whomever and with whatever they needed.

When they first arrived at YD they inquired if there was anything we needed, I stated that we were short on ammunition because our CoC literally stated "We were not in a combat zone." This specific officer believed this and would only allow us to carry the bare minimum of ammunition regardless of the fire fights we had already been in. The SF leader led us into a metal conex full of weapons and munitions telling us to take whatever we needed. Before us was a collection of almost every type of rifles, pistols, and explosives. We were never without the ammunition and supplies that we needed again.

FIRE IN THE VALLEY

One of our long walks led us into a fire fight that had an enduring impact on me. My ongoing struggle with my Christian faith and my attitude toward our Muslim enemies was pushed to the edge during this mission. We were moving down from our temporary base through a village market on our way to a girls' school a few miles ahead. While passing thru the market we dismounted and shopped our way through it. This tactic was much less disruptive to the locals, winning hearts and minds when we spent money on food, fuel, etc.

I did not expect trouble while passing through the market since standard experience was that the enemy would not shoot at you with women and children present. While discussing the price of diesel with a local vendor I was startled by the sound of rapid gunfire coming from the tree line. I also heard the sound of bullets hitting metal vehicles, a sound I learned all too well from my previous tour to Iraq. I heard the alarming sound of people screaming as they fell to the ground or ran into the buildings. One of the most vivid sights was the look I saw from one older man; I caught his look of desperation. I became angry that these cowards would place these innocent people in harm's way, using them as shields. This was Iraq all over again.

All this happened in a split second, as I was moving with my Afghan soldiers and my (SF) team. We quickly determined that two Afghan soldiers had been shot and our medic was on them instantly as they dragged them out of the street. We left a rear security team at the market and began to move around the buildings toward the creek. We were now in an elevated position and saw the enemy, approximately twelve men, moving into the village below. When I saw them I hated them. I wanted to not just shoot them, I wanted to kill them. My team consisted of two Afghan squads, two SF and an interpreter. Another team began a flanking movement to the west; the north and east was a steep mountain range, so we were trying to push them into a box ravine.

After we crossed the creek and climbed the embankment into a field looking out toward the village, we were engaged by small arms fire. We moved to cover and returned fire as they retreated. We took off running, crossing the field in two wedge formations. As we closed in on a building they opened fire again over a four-foot wall. There was a mother and two small children lying down in front of the wall. While under fire, two Afghan soldiers grabbed the children and led their mother to our rear.

As I approached the wall, I saw a man trying to scale another wall. Shots were fired at him as he disappeared over the wall. I knew that he was hit because of the way he reeled over the wall. When I reached the other side of the wall, he was gone, but there were traces of blood where he had hit the ground. There were several other enemies doing this as well. They had become disorganized and seemed to be in a panic. They were used to a quick shoot-and-hide, they did not anticipate us, and we literally ran them down. They were running now holding their AKs with one hand, shooting randomly in our direction as we moved forward with controlled fire.

I was not sure how far I had run, but I was amazed that we were all still together. Shooting now began to be heard in front of us and to our sides as the enemy was trying to disperse fire to find a way out. We pressed hard now running as fast as we could, we did not want to lose them at the river. I remember feeling the adrenaline rush, thinking I wanted to catch them so I could kill them.

As I passed by a building, the enemy was less than fifty yards to my right and opened fire on my Afghan soldiers and me. I turned my rifle in that direction and fired reflexively, as did my Afghans. There were two enemies directly in front of us. The closest man was hit with a three round burst from an ANA soldier, and I saw a spray of blood behind him as he went down. The other appeared to be wounded as he disappeared into the woods.

As I approached the downed enemy, he looked like a gutted deer. I didn't hesitate at that site as I was too far into the zone; it wasn't until later that that memory began to haunt me. We pursued the last man into the woods until we came to the river. We followed his blood trail, for a hundred yards until it disappeared into the water. We were getting too far away from the main element and could find ourselves in a bad way if we did not regroup soon. We made our way back to the village without further action.

The area was finally secured and medivac had been called for the wounded. We regrouped back at our base for an AAR. The Afghan commander and my counterpart approached me with a smile and gave me the shell casing from one of my rounds fired. He told me to keep it for good luck, and then he smiled and said I had fought well. One of the SF grinned slightly and quietly said, "Good job." That was one of the proudest moments of my life. I was considered a soldier by these Mujahidin and SF soldiers, not bad for a NG/teacher.

Later that night the Afghans came to the SF and said that the locals had brought one of the wounded to us for help. This was not uncommon; many of the locals were not Taliban but were forced at gun point to fight for them. They also knew that United States soldiers would take care of their wounded. When I saw him, I recognized him as the man that was shot going over the wall. He looked to be a teenager; his torso and back were soaked in blood. The medics worked on him as we called for a medivac, I remember him crying out Allah's name. We made eye contact momentarily, his eyes were dark but not angry as I would have thought, just frightened and lost. He died as we looked at each other, "He's gone, lost too much blood," said the medic, and the villagers who had brought him took him away from us.

The range of emotions I felt that day and later that night were conflicting. I had been angry, scared, desperate, proud and ashamed. The next few days the Afghans kept patting me on the back saying, "Good SGT." The SF told me I had done a good job and said they wanted me to work with them for the rest of my tour; they put me in for my CIB and other commendations for later actions.

I know I did the right thing by protecting myself, and my comrades. I knew that by killing them they would not harm another United States soldier; I knew all that. So why did I feel nauseous when I thought about it? When I smell gun smoke from a fired weapon I think of that day, and others.

CHAPTER NINETEEN

BACK TO SCHOOL

Throughout the remainder of my tour we engaged in a number of short- and long-term missions. Some lasted a few days, while others, weeks and months. My final mission was both a turning point for me and the crowning achievement of my time in Afghanistan. To provide some context, it should be noted that the Taliban was adamantly opposed to education for girls. Their position was that the only sanctioned role for women was as wives and mothers; any education outside of the home is at best a distraction and at worst is dishonoring to Islam.

A new girls' school had been built to replace the one that had previously been destroyed by the Taliban. We received intelligence that the Taliban were threatening girls and their families if their daughters attempted to attend that school. This intelligence came through the ANA military directly. We discussed possible options and the best response came from A-Top himself. He stated that we would move his ANA into the school and force the Taliban to move against him. That idea was brilliant; the girls would not need the school since Afghan children only attend school from spring through fall, the winter being too harsh to travel.

I looked forward to being away from the Flag Pole again; I needed to be in the fight not facilitating some ICT's career. We did indeed move into the school, which was modern by Afghan standards, stone and mortar walls, concrete roof and actual glass in the windows with intermittent electricity, yet without furniture, indoor plumbing or school supplies of any kind. Mooremart would address the school supply issue rather quickly and with great success.

Our arrival was most definitely a surprise to the enemy in that area based upon their response. We moved in and immediately established a secure perimeter using the school wall and firing positions on top of the building. Before the sun set on the first day a group of young boys arrived with a male "teacher" telling us that this was their school and we must leave. This lie was obvious (even to us Americans), but we let the ANA handle it. A-Top berated this teacher openly accusing him of being Taliban and a liar! The teacher and the boys walked off in a hurry and my interpreter explained what had transpired. A-Top publicly insulted this man knowing that it would end this charade; moreover, it would force the enemy to attack, providing us with the opportunity to do what we do best—pick a fight!

This strategy always worked well instead of wasting time playing cat-and-mouse with an enemy that could blend in with civilians. We would create situations that begged him to come to us and on our terms. Adding to this tactic was the fact that working with the SF meant that we had resources that most Line Units (LU) did not. Along with long range weapons and dedicated air support we also had high tech intelligence. The enemy was communicating with standard hand held radios which we were able to intercept. Our interpreters would translate their plans to us in real time; so we pretended to retire for the night knowing that they had planned on attacking us. We hid inside the building while listening to their communications as they moved into position on the ridge line above the village and along the river bank.

One of the few humorous transmissions we did hear came when our interpreter began laughing and explained that one of the enemies was complaining about the freezing cold and was going home if they did not give the order to attack soon. We all got a chuckle for a moment until we heard them give the order and all hell broke loose. The school was obviously not built with force security in mind; we were surrounded by mountains which gave the enemy the high ground advantage. The building had one floor with a long hall ending with large doorways.

The enemy had sighted these doors and immediately bullets were skipping down the long hallway ricocheting off the walls. It was then that we realized that we had to run down that hall to get outside. Fortunately, the ANA were already in position outside on top of the perimeter wall returning fire. I waited for a short lull in the bullets, and then ran for the door. We were able to get outside and join the ANA on the wall.

These night time attacks continued as our immediate plan was to not strike back but try to draw in the enemy. A-Top stated that they were probing our defenses, trying to see what we had for weapons and what our intentions were. Our intelligence revealed that they were massing troops around us for the hope to overrun our position. In that case we could not call in air support thereby denying us that tactical advantage.

The decision was made to form two strike teams combining ANA and United States soldiers. The idea being that they would not expect us to strike out at them at this point and would be caught off guard when we did. We did make the most of it and it worked like a charm, completely catching them on their heels sending them running.

One particular event demonstrated the stark difference between Arab Muslims and those in Afghanistan. In Iraq, the enemy openly used mosques as a base of operation with impunity. Our American command would not allow us to enter those buildings but the Iraqi soldiers would not go in after the enemy either. Imagine our frustration, knowing exactly where the enemy is but not being allowed to deal with them over religious/political sensitivities.

This was not so in Afghanistan. Though we were still not allowed to enter their mosques, the Afghans would not hesitate to do so.

The ANA were furious that Muslims would use their place of prayer as a way to hide from us. During one of the enemy's attacks we sent out two strike teams, one toward the ravine leading to the river and the other pushed to flank them at the far side of the village. That was when both teams stopped at a mosque. Knowing that the enemy had retreated inside, I remained outside while A-Top entered. I expected to hear shooting but only heard shouting followed by A-Top coming out with a few Afghan men at gun point.

These were local villagers who had fought with the enemy, but only under threat of death, which is a common tactic in Afghanistan. They had decided to run away from the Taliban and seek refuge in their mosque. A-Top spoke with them sternly and released them to return to the mosque. He stated that he knew they were telling the truth and we would lose faith with the villagers if we took them into custody. Yet before releasing them, they did provide us with some critical intelligence that we were able to act upon immediately.

All of our team and the ANA returned unharmed (which was impressive) and by the time we were finished the enemy had all but abandoned that valley. Throughout the time that followed we had several other engagements at the school itself as well as the surrounding villages. A detachment of ANA was assigned to build a base of its own near the school, and by spring the girls were attending classes again. The success of this mission had such a profound and immediate impact on the local population there that it became the crowning point of my tour. Knowing that these girls were able to attend school without threat of violence was something that I could always look back at and see an obvious reason for my being there.

HEARTS AND MINDS

Our time at the school was also a time of getting to know the ANA better, as well as reaching out to the local villagers. One of our most successful events was bringing medical aid out to that school. A number of medical personnel were brought out for a few days, administering to men in one tent and women with children in another. Afghans from miles away walked for days to get there in order to have medical attention, the first time for many.

One cultural issue we had to deal with was that women were not allowed to be examined by any doctor regardless of gender. We addressed this by having the Afghan moms take their younger children in to see female medical personnel with an interpreter. After tending to the needs of the children they would ask the mother how she was doing and within the privacy of that tent they were able to tend to her needs as well. It is situations like these that helped me to see these people not as Muslims but as families that needed help. It also helped me make sense of my time there, soften my heart and begin the process of healing.

MEN LINED UP TO SEE THE DOCTOR,
THE WOMEN WITH CHILDREN WERE SEEN AWAY FROM THE MEN.

END OF TOUR

My tour in Afghanistan ended on a high note, but with some reservations as well. I had come a long way from when I had first arrived believing that all Muslims were like those that I had met in Iraq or worse. I was now at a place where not only did I have a greater appreciation of Muslims in general, but I considered some close friends. These Afghan Muslim soldiers had shared their food with me, talked with me about home, family, politics and religion. At times they had literally saved my life without hesitation, just because I was their friend; my religion or cultural background was irrelevant to them.

I was especially moved when A-Top himself stated that he was happy for me to return to my family but was sad that I was leaving. He actually asked me to return with my wife and family to assume a position as teacher for his village. He offered a home, money and food along with protection for us as well. Here was a Muslim leader who thought enough of me that he wanted me, a Christian westerner, to teach his very own children.

I thanked him for his friendship and faith in me in offering me such an important position. Though I would have to decline (at least for the immediate future), I hoped that when my own children were grown I might return with God's blessings. To this day I correspond with some of my former interpreters who are fortunate enough to have access to the internet. I will always hold my Afghan friends close to my heart and I pray for God's protection for them.

CHAPTER TWENTY

HEADED HOME

Captain Casey and I left Yellow Dog for the last time amid mixed emotions. Some of the American soldiers that I served with had accepted an offer for a six month extension. This was spring of 2006 and with the war in Iraq and Afghanistan going on the Army was pushing hard for soldiers to extend. The Army began offering re-enlistment bonuses and a choice of duty station if we would stay.

I would be lying if I did not admit that I contemplated staying. It was easy to rationalize why it would be beneficial to me and my family if I did stay. The money was good and would help my family's financial situation. My sense of service also pulled me in that direction as I was well established with the ANA and would be a tremendous asset to any new team coming in.

Personally, I was at the top of my game. In my own mind I mattered and believed that my presence on the battlefield made a significant difference.

I walked humbly but with purpose and distinction, I was a warrior among warriors. I was sought by those in SF groups for my participation with their missions; I had never experienced anything like that at home. Other than my immediate family, what did I actually have to go home too? Yet I knew my wife and kids missed and needed me, so home is where I was headed.

Near the end of our tour we were directed to write a narrative of our missions for the possibility of being awarded medals for our exemplary service. I will state again that some of the officers I worked with were honorable, such as Captain Casey. Others were less so. I discovered through another NCO friend at YD that a letter commending myself and others on my team for our service during a particular mission was forwarded to our CoC. When they received it, it was read and immediately thrown into the trash rather than placed into our permanent records and added to our narratives for a possible award. My friend saw this happen and retrieved the letter, which was a commendation by a SF unit I served with on their letter head. Needless to say I received nothing of note from this specific CoC. I was however awarded a Combat Infantry Badge (CIB) from the SF unit to which I was attached. That recognition from them is worth more to me than any other award I could have received. In all honesty, the greatest award I received was the admiration from the American and ANA soldiers with whom I served!

SSG MOORE AND SSG COPELAND "BIG TOE"
WITH OUR MM T-SHIRT AND A FOOT OF AFGHAN SNOW.

Captain Casey and I moved back onto our initial staging base and were reunited with our original War Eagle's team. It was good to see them all again, and even better to know that they had survived their tours as well. We shared war stories, most tending to be on the humorous side. By now we were beginning the psychological transition out of the combat zone and knew that the darker side of the war would be better left behind. The demobilization process began here with the packing and turning in of gear and weapons. The day finally came when we boarded the plane and made the long cold flight over the mountains of Afghanistan for one last time.

A few days of flights and we were back at Fort Hood for our final processing out of active duty. The War Eagles spent a few nights celebrating the success of our tours and the reality that most of us would never serve together again. We were all from different states and it was unlikely that we would see each other after this. The last official task we had together was getting to the airport and dispersing to our various gates for the final flight home. My initial interaction with the Transportation Security Agency (TSA) was a bad omen for things to come. I was traveling home in my desert uniform with a large group of soldiers when the agent advised me that that I was "randomly chosen" for a full search and that I must remove my boots and belt. My blood pressure immediately began to boil as I asked him if he did not recognize the uniform of his own country and that I had returned from my second tour fighting the terrorists for whom he was supposedly looking. His snide response was "Timothy McVeigh was in the military."

I lost it! That statement is commonly used by some to denigrate the United States military in an attempt to imply that all veterans are suspects of domestic terrorism.

It is highly offensive to veterans to be associated with him and we do not take it lightly!

I was immediately saved by some fellow NCOs who were in line behind me. They intervened and convinced this agent's supervisor that he did not want the arrest of a United States soldier on the evening news. I was moved to my boarding gate where I entered my plane. I have come to learn that when someone starts a conversation with "I support the troops but..." they are full of it! It sounds more like an excuse for having never served in the military than the moral authority to criticize and diminish every sacrifice made by veterans today.

This type of response usually comes from those who do not know what we actually do while serving in combat and are only parroting some politically correct mantra.

I landed in NH with no fanfare, media or parades; just Raquel, which was perfect. Since I had deployed alone from NH, there was no mass movement of soldiers to be greeted. In fact after I was home for a week I called the NH Guard and reported that I was back from Afghanistan and inquired as to my next move. Later that week I arrived at headquarters where I was met by a Command Sergeant Major (CSM). He was glad to see me home, in one piece and was apologetic that no one had met me at the airport. He was not happy that they had dropped the ball and felt that every soldier should be met when returning from a combat zone. Although I did notify the appropriate personnel that I was returning, I did not want to throw anyone under the bus. I was just happy to be home.

I met with the officer who had gone to bat for me and he was obviously thrilled to see that I had finished my tour. He wanted me to know that he had kept tabs on my progress and was impressed with the reports that did circulate back to our NG HQ about my service. He also informed me that there had been some restructuring of his unit and that I would need to look for another one within the NH Guard. My initial thought was to transfer back to the Mountain Infantry unit, with which I had started my Army career. However, I was informed that our state was forming a new MP unit and they were looking for experienced NCOs to help build its core leadership. I transferred to the MPs which consisted of a handful of NCOs and less than a dozen soldiers. This decision would lead me to a place that the Lord had prepared for me.

BACK IN THE WORLD

I returned to my home, family and work as if nothing had happened, nothing had changed in me. Being away from my family for over a year had a far greater impact on me and them than I could have anticipated. My two youngest children had grown almost twelve inches each in the fifteen months I had been gone; yet more importantly, I had children when I left and I returned to teenagers.

When soldiers deploy we expect the world freezes in place as if the day we return to our home will be the day after we had left. Reality can be an abrupt wakeup call! I have learned that the healthiest way to approach these reunions is to anticipate change and by maintaining frequent dialog with my wife. During my tour I knew that Raquel had not shared everything with me in regards to the kids and their difficulties. In hindsight, I would have asked her to get me up to speed during the demobilization process so I would have been better prepared for the inevitable tsunami of "being back."

This sense of the world having frozen in place also applied to the world at large. In our high-tech world it is amazing how much our culture had shifted. Teaching was no exception. I returned to the public school I had been employed at prior to my last deployment. When I returned to work, rather then resume teaching my own class, I was placed in a temporary office position in order to allow the long-term substitute to complete the year. At first I thought this was a good idea until I realized that the administration did not know what to do with the "combat veteran." This treatment only served to make me feel even more alienated. It was as if I was a ghost walking the halls with no real purpose or destination. I eventually resigned my teaching position and acquired a full-time position with the NHNG. Although this position meant that I spent three to four days per week away from home, I did feel like I belonged, surrounded by familiar sights and faces.

It is said that combat vets are usually haunted by feelings of regret and guilt. Regret for those things that they did not do and guilt for those that they did, and I was no exception. I had regret for not doing more to eliminate the power of our enemy on the field and at home—the lure of extended deployments thinking, "There was always one more enemy to kill." My guilt was conflicted based upon the death of our enemies, either I felt bad about their death or I did not. At times it was difficult to distinguish between the two and which one was a heavier burden to carry. I believed at that time I would not deploy again and that eventually I would resolve those feelings. Honestly, all I could manage was to bury them deeper along with so many other painful thoughts. So I went home with a smile because being with my wife and kids was all that mattered and that would make all else seem irrelevant.

Near the end of my deployment I began to think of how great it would be to be home again, with my wife, children and family. Yet I found the reality to be anti-climactic and stressful. My wife had to make decisions in my absence that I did not understand, and I had to let go of any disagreement I might have had. I found the biggest stumbling block for me was coming from a position of authority and making things happen. I had come from a world where most of the pressing issues were black and white to one of levels of gray. It is at times like this that many veterans long to return to the combat zone, where we at least mattered and knew the rules.

I had no plans to redeploy, so I was advised to go to the Veterans Administration hospital and file for a disability status based upon injuries I had incurred during my prior tours. During those tours I had been exposed to multiple explosions and a vehicle roll over that had resulted in several concussions and of course some level of PTSD. The result was a combined disability rating of 50% overall (in VA jargon, "50% connected").

NEVER SAY NEVER

I had joined the MP unit for a couple of good reasons. To be part of the building of a new unit would have certain challenges that I would welcome. It would also place me in a good position to be promoted as the unit grew to a full strength company. Finally, I believed that belonging to a small start-up unit would ensure that I would not be deployed again. I knew that if I went back to the infantry company I would eventually be deployed. The consensus was that it would be a few years before we would be deployable.

Well, the day did come when the decision was made by those far above my pay grade to deploy our platoon size unit to Iraq. Our platoon was to be attached to a company from another state to build up their numbers. Most of the other NCOs and officers saw this as a bad idea on several levels. The command structure would be a headache at the least, not to mention trying to blend two different state NG units into one for the purpose of deploying to a combat zone. Yet this was the order, so it was our job to make it happen quickly and successfully.

I was approached by the command who reiterated that due to my recent return from Afghanistan I was not expected to deploy again. Although my initial gut response was a desire to deploy again, I was still getting back on track with my family. I spent the next few months preparing the platoon size unit for their pending deployment.

Yet my effort to help these young soldiers was pulling me toward deploying again.

The decision to volunteer to deploy again did not initiate with me however. My wife attended a unit promotion ceremony and watched me working with those young troops. Before we left the NG Armory parking lot Raquel stated, "You need to go, they need you more than I do." This took me totally by surprise, since she and I had had several conversations on all of the turmoil that she dealt with while I was deployed.

I told her that I did not want to put her and the younger children on the back burner again, that they needed me home. She agreed that it would be difficult again, more so now that they were coming of age, but she felt that the Holy Spirit had moved her toward that decision. Raquel was not overly religious by any definition, if she said that the Holy Spirit moved her then that was gospel for me.

I met with the unit leadership and expressed my intent to deploy. Their reaction was more positive then I had expected. In fact one response was, "This is huge, and these troops really need you." That has always stuck with me, not in a conceited way of course, it was just another moment of me realizing "I matter again."

CHAPTER TWENTY-ONE

THE BEGINNING OF THE END: GROUNDHOG DAY

"The more things change, the more they stay the same," would be an understatement for the beginning of the end of my military career. By the time our platoon was formed we had a very good balance of old and young troops and seasoned leadership. When I learned that we were to spend ninety days at yet another mobilization site I just had to laugh. The Army will spend money and time to prepare experienced soldiers how to do what they already know. Three months of irrelevant training to which I reminded the troops, "Just check the block and we'll be in the sandbox before you know it." To add insult to injury (or just Murphy's Law) the mobilization location was in NJ in January for our first tour, then we would spend three months training in southern Mississippi through June, July and August. We were either freezing or gasping for air in one-hundred-percent humidity.

Yet being in a leadership position and responsible for so many young soldiers forced me to think way beyond myself. I needed to prepare my soldiers for surviving in a combat zone. As the Platoon SGT (PS), I had two tasks ahead: to take care of the troops and cover the Platoon Leader's back (PL). I wrote earlier of learning from good as well as bad leadership, and the one thing that stands out to me is that good leaders motivate their men to do what must be done. A bad leader manipulates men to do what they want done for their own benefit.

I will not spend a lot of time discussing the mobilization experience as in the years since my first tour the only thing that had changed was that we had gone from frostbite to heat stroke. I had hoped that those in command would have learned to do mobilization better. Just as it was during my first mobilization where the troops were not allowed to go to sick call for a cold weather injury, now it was true in reverse. The troops were not allowed to go to sick call for a hot weather injury. We were required to attend the same inaccurate, politically correct lectures on the Muslim culture.

One of the worst results of a lack of organization by the PP was my troops having to repeat training. Paperwork would be lost and those in charge of the training would require those on the missing list to repeat the class. That gets especially aggravating when the training is going through the gas chamber for the third time. There were the usual headaches and frustrations yet we had our share of fun as well. The humorous side of our time with this southern NG unit was trying to assimilate Northern New England "Yankees" with Southern "Rebels." Our new battle buddies referred to us as Canadians, stating that we lived so far north that we were not even from America, to which our troops responded with Civil War jabs, but at the end of the tour we were a tight unit.

"WHEELS UP!" SFC Moore & SSG Penney waiting to load plane for Iraq.

A VERY DIFFERENT WAR

Iraq had changed, or at least how we were fighting the war had changed. During my first tour, which was more like the Wild West, we lived with the bare minimums and were allowed to engage the enemy whenever necessary. Big Army had arrived now; this was a kinder, gentler war, where instead of "driving like you stole it" we crept down the roads of Baghdad.

My squads drove so slowly that Iraqis would literally jump out in front of our trucks hoping to get hit in order to receive payment from the United States for injuries sustained from the military. Payment was often made, though there were never any "real" injuries!

During our first tour whenever the enemy fired rockets at us or used human shields we dealt with them swiftly and severely. This always ended with the same result, they stopped any actions that did not work or might get them killed. Yet this time we were to spend the entire tour being bombarded on a daily basis while hiding in bunkers waiting for the bad men to stop.

A most disheartening day occurred during one such attack when one of my troops told me that he felt like a coward. "Why don't we shoot back, surely we can target them?" I advised him that we could not fire back at them because these courageous warriors of Islam were launching their rockets and mortars from a school yard. The enemy did this just hoping we would fire back and injure some Iraqi children, what wonderful press coverage that would make. He responded with, "Then let's send squads out on foot, surely we can run them down! I'll go and so will the rest of the platoon." I admired his courage and sincerity and told him so. I also agreed with his tactics, since I knew first hand that his stated response would work.

Yet I reminded him that we were constrained by those in command and had to work within that reality. The reality that some commanders are either too far removed from the situation to appreciate what is happening or they are just too afraid to make a decision that might go wrong. This is sometimes called the "paralysis-of-analysis" or "command freeze." I also need to recognize the pressure these commanders were under from their own CoC. This would not be the first American war lost by politicians in Washington, D.C., who were worried more about short term election results than a long term peace through a hard fought victory.

It was at these times that I longed for the freedom of Afghanistan or the open road of Iraq being far enough away from the Flag Pole to deal with the enemy immediately and severely. Being boxed in on base was not how I was built and was another aggravation that I had to deal with while maintaining the morale of the troops.

The bright side of the tour was the living conditions compared to my first, where fourteen men lived in one room or slept on top of their trucks. No internet or cell phones, one cold shower for thirty-five men. This tour, each soldier had a room with heat, AC and Internet service with one other soldier. There was a trailer of hot showers and a chow hall that defied description. This is not to downplay the sacrifice and danger our company had to endure every day as they left the base. Working outside the wire is never a good time and is potentially deadly. It is just an observation of how much the war in Iraq had changed.

SWAMP LIFE

Soldiers can always find the lighter side of hardship. The fact that we were being mortared on a regular basis just became our reality. There were occasions when the enemy would park a truck on the road outside our base with rockets preloaded on the bed. After parking the truck and aiming by line of sight they would hide in a nearby building. When ready they would launch the rockets electronically. This enabled them to evade detection and film the attack without becoming targets themselves.

It was not uncommon for these preset rockets to malfunction either self-detonating or not firing at all. The base Explosive Ordnance Disposal (EOD) team would respond and their mission was to disarm and dispose of the explosives from a safe location. At times this was not possible due to the unstable condition of the explosives found. The next best option was to blow the rocket in place with the intent of it self-destructing.

This is not an exact science; therefore the explosion might shower our base with shrapnel. Not enough to injure anyone but enough for us to joke about "EOD is shooting at us again." This joke was no longer funny when the EOD managed explosion caused some of the rockets to actually launch and impact inside our base. Thankfully no one was injured, but one rocket did impact the motor pool (where our vehicles are parked and maintained).

The explosion ruptured an underground eighteen-inch water main pipeline. The result was an enormous amount of water being pumped into the motor pool and spreading quickly. It was obvious to those of us who lived in that area of the base that this would be out of control soon if that pipe was not repaired. Reports were sent up to the base command but response was slow at best. Unfortunately we were situated on the low end of the base which caused the water to flood our living area.

The adage "out of sight out of mind" fits this situation perfectly. The base command did not see what we were actually living with therefore did not have a sense of urgency to fix it. The entire area became a swamp of the worst kind. The water around our rooms was eighteen-inches deep, inches away from the door. The water carried everything you would expect from that part of the world and worse. The dark water was literally a flowing sewer that we were forced to walk through for days-on-end.

The unfortunate reality of the military is that some in command will not address an issue unless it impacts them directly. Whether that stems from a misplaced theory that living in miserable conditions toughens the troops or just from a different set of priorities. It became clear to some of us that nothing would change until it directly impacted those who could make it happen.

It was obvious that the only thing keeping the water contained in our area was the crest of the road. Late one night it is rumored that a few NCOs went out with shovels and dug a trench across the road.

This opened the way for the nasty water to flow freely into other areas of the base. Before the day was over men and equipment were put to the task of closing the pipe and pumping the sewer water off the base.

"JUST ANOTHER DAY IN PARADISE"

Most of the soldiers in the company knew of my background as a Christian, a fact that either led either to opportunities for evangelizing or hateful comments directed at me. I referenced paradise when engaging in small talk with other soldiers; it was a good way to open a door for evangelism. I could discuss the historical significance of our supposed proximity to the Garden of Eden, which on occasion led to an open discussion of spiritual significance.

Yet being back in a combat zone in a Muslim country with all of the familiar sights sounds and of course smells was a challenge. Since my time serving with the Afghan soldiers had taught me so much about their faith and culture I was becoming torn again with the memories of my first tour to Iraq. The horrendous things I saw there were being repeated again. Using school children as human shields only served to stir my disdain for our enemy, yet I believed that I had overcome my hatred for those Muslims who would do such things.

My memory of where I had been spiritually was still very clear, and I did not want to go back there again. I spent my mornings and evenings in prayer and devotions, I can say that the struggle I fought to maintain my relationship with Jesus was definitely a spiritual one. I believe that Satan threw as much at me spiritually as well as physically and emotionally to cause me to ruin my testimony. I am not claiming to be some modern saint or holy man but in a stressful situation like a combat zone, especially when men and women are serving far away from home, temptations are ever present. Yet I have always been aware that if younger soldiers were looking to me for leadership both professionally and spiritually, I would be under attack by the Evil One. There would be no greater victory for Satan than to cause me to fall in front of so many who were still searching for spiritual truth, and I did not want to be the cause for them turning from that path.

My own experience over the years has been that the closer I try to walk with God the more Satan throws at me. I definitely felt him manipulating my deeper distrust and hatred for our Muslim enemies, so I worked to recognize those occasions. Just like in human combat, if you are expecting to be shot at then prepare for it, if you do not then you are an easy target. Interestingly enough, the harder he pushed me the more I leaned on God for every aspect of my life.

I share the following incident only to demonstrate how crazy things can get when you are under attack from Satan, and why it is vitally important to keep a clear mind that is focused on God's truth. On more than one occasion a young female soldier (not from my unit) would come to my room alone, late at night, crying and wanting to talk. Being immediately suspicious and skeptical, I would not allow any women into my room alone and insisted that we get another female NCO to talk with her. That was always followed by weeping pleas, and the individual stating they only wanted to talk with me alone, while they attempted to acquire a hug from me. I am not claiming that I am made of stone, but along with my love and commitment to my wife and family and my desire to be right before God, I am also not that gullible.

I was not gullible enough to believe that a young woman, who was currently serving with hundreds of young male soldiers, suddenly found a man old enough to be her father so attractive that she needed to seek me out late at night. Yet it always ended the same; I would insist on getting a female NCO and the young weeping soldier would immediately stop crying and reply with "forget it," and stomp off with an attitude. I obviously do not believe that they were agents of Satan doing his bidding, but I do know that the more I tried to be right the more temptation landed in my lap. Unfortunately adultery and other assorted violations of military regulations seemed to be epidemic on that base. Perhaps some soldiers sought to ease their own conviction by causing me to fail spiritually. Fortunately this type of solicitation ended as quickly as it had begun.

YOU CAN'T FIX STUPID

A wise CSM told me that the adage "Rank has its privileges" should only apply when those with rank have met their obligations. He continued with "Leading troops in combat will be the most stressful time of your life, and it will be the most rewarding as well." I would understand his meaning more during this last tour than ever before. As a Platoon SGT I soon realized that herding cats might have been an easier profession. Yet there were many times that I was never more proud of any group of soldiers than I was of those of my last tour.

The title, "You Can't Fix Stupid" is not meant to be insulting, but it does help explain what those in leadership must deal with throughout their careers. It will also help to explain some of the stress that I was under during this last tour. The greatest stressor of all was being held accountable for the actions of fifty other soldiers twenty-four hours a day. Yet that is how the military is supposed to work, which is why it does work so well.

Micromanagement in the military does not work; soldiers must be trained, motivated and directed. After that they will make decisions that will reflect well or poorly on their leadership, and all I could do was wait for one or the other. My NCO CoC was directly through the First SGT of our company. When my troops screwed up my commander called me to account, not them. In fact there is a saying in the Army for this, "When you screw up you screw up your CoC."

This played out on a regular basis, although not because my troops were screw-ups. It is just human nature to make mistakes times fifty. I would cringe when I would hear "3-7" (my call sign) on the radio either from TOP or HQ. Some mistakes can be addressed with some retraining and motivation. For instance each platoon was required to supply a few soldiers each day to work for the base command. This could be tower duty, dining hall or supervising local national day workers. My platoon went through a period of time where some would over sleep. That meant that I would receive a call on the radio, which the entire company could hear, that one of my troops had failed to report. This was inevitably followed by a call from TOP.

After a few failed attempts to correct this problem myself I decided to hold their immediate supervisors responsible. I advised each team leader that if their soldier failed to report to their duty station I would send the team leader instead. I only had to do that one time, I rolled the team leader out of bed on his day off and he worked the day for that soldier. It never happened again throughout my platoon.

I had another soldier (who I will name "Ouch" since he tended to break things) whose biggest problem was his desire to work as little as possible when that work was not combat-related. In his mind, his only job was to ride around manning a machine gun and shoot at bad guys; anything else was beneath him. That is not how the military works and fighting that system never ends well. The day came when Ouch came running up to me looking distressed. I knew this would not be good. He stated that when he parked his Humvee (a seven-ton armored vehicle) on the wash ramp he failed to engage the emergency brake and to chock the tires, all mandatory safety procedures. This is what happens when soldiers regard any work beneath them; they don't take it seriously or pay attention to detail.

His Humvee rolled down the ramp (with no driver) and careened across a parking lot full of people and eventually crashed into a chain link fence. Thankfully no one was injured, but the fence was literally wrapped around the Humvee, pulling the poles out of the ground—concrete base and all. As I stood there staring in disbelief he said in all seriousness, "This is on me SGT Moore," to which I replied, "No, it's not; it's on me!" I no sooner finished that statement when I heard TOP on the radio, "3-7, report to me now!"

Some of these events are more humorous now than they were then. I will not forget that after the Humvee was removed, the fence maintained the shape of the Humvee. One of my fellow NCOs jokingly commented that it looked like some expensive display of modern art. I had to agree with him.

The most distressing screw-up and the name sake of this section came out of nowhere. While discussing the work schedule with my NCOs, we suddenly heard one gun shot fired down the alley from us. We froze for a moment thinking we didn't just hear that. Until we heard a loud scream, more from panic than from pain. We ran down the alley to find the screaming soldier (I'll call Frenchy) with blood covering his arm which another soldier was holding to slow the bleeding. Prior experience had taught me that if Frenchy did not calm down he might bleed out. The faster his heart raced the faster it would pump blood out of his arm.

I grabbed his face with both hands and yelled, "Frenchy, am I going to let you die?"

To which he replied, "No, SGT Moore!"

"Then sit down and shut up!"

Frenchy sat down ceased his screaming and allowed the medics to work on him.

My first thought was that Frenchy had shot himself, which was my first question.

The soldier spoke up and stated, "I shot him."

My heart sank. It was bad enough for a soldier to accidently shoot himself, but when one soldier shoots another soldier, everything changes and it escalates to a criminal investigation.

I secured the scene taking custody of the weapon and the shooter. My entire command responded to my location and Frenchy was taken to the base hospital. Frenchy was stabilized and returned to the United States for treatment. The investigation determined that there was no malicious intent and the shooting was a negligent action. Before this was over, I was ordered to travel across Baghdad to stand before the Brigade CSM and then the Division CSM to give account of the shooting.

Those unfamiliar with the military might ask why I was held responsible when I had no immediate control over these soldiers' actions. Yet I understood that as the PS I was accountable for the actions of my soldiers. I also understood that whatever came out of the CSM's mouth my only response was either "Yes, CSM," or "No,

CSM," period. The Brigade CSM verbally tore me up one side and down the other with TOP and the Battalion CSM present and then dismissed me. I then appeared before the Division CSM this time alone. I thought for sure I would have no "ass" left after this meeting. Considering the rank of the Division CSM, I knew that he answered "only to God" and now I was standing in front of his desk. He read the file for a moment then asked for my account of what happened. I spoke of what I knew to be true as he sat and stared at me for a moment. He then ordered me to sit down and stated, "You can't fix stupid, SGT Moore!" I replied, "No, CSM, I can't." I was dismissed and returned to my base. It was events such as these that led me to sleepless nights ever waiting for the radio to sound off with "3-7, 3-7."

DEATH FROM ABOVE

It began as just another day in Baghdad, up at zero-dark thirty to send my squads outside the wire for another long day of work. This began my routine which was followed by meeting with the CoC for daily updates and then off to the gym. I had returned from the gym when I heard the all too familiar alarm blaring over the base, "Incoming, incoming." This alarm gave us a three to five second warning that we had incoming rockets and mortars.

I jumped up from my desk and ran outside heading toward the concrete bunker. Most of my troops were outside the wire already so I had only a handful on base. I'll be the first to admit that we had become complacent in regards to these attacks. The danger was very real even though the attacks happened almost daily, rarely resulting in any loss of life. Typically the rockets were fired randomly at our base hoping to hit something of significance. Yet these attacks were never a waste of resources by the enemy because they worked well at general harassment and at lowering troop morale.

I was the last soldier entering the bunker as I was directing the others to move further inside. Our bunker had never been completed so it was actually wide open at one end. Just as I was stepping in I saw the first round impact the motor pool parking lot and I immediately knew we were in trouble. I knew this because it was not a rocket fired at random but rather a smoke round which is used for directing following fire. This meant that there was a Forward Observer (FO) on or overlooking our base directing the enemies fire based upon where the smoke landed. The following rounds proved me right.

The trailers that we lived in were built in rows all evenly distanced apart with bunkers positioned at the end of each row. During these alarms all of the soldiers would immediately run for the bunker which was where the rounds began to impact. It was discovered later that an Iraqi national that worked on our base had paced out the distance of the bunkers and had forwarded that intelligence to the enemy. During the attack he was positioned on top of a building on base with a cell phone literally directing the enemy fire at our bunkers.

Much of what happened after that point forward was a blur, but from what I do recall (and from what I was told by other soldiers) this is what occurred. While explosions were taking place in front of the other bunkers one rocket exploded directly behind me. The force of this explosion swept over me like a wave and took me off my feet. For that moment in time I felt like I was floating while my back was on fire. I was in and out of consciousness from that point forward.

I remember my vision returning and seeing another NCO kneeling over me talking to me but I could not hear him clearly, he was trying to assess my injuries. My sense of hearing was muffled at first but eventually would return sporadically. I could hear other soldiers near me calling out to each other, some in pain and others trying to take control of the immediate area. When I became more coherent I attempted to sit up but discovered that I was partially paralyzed due to the trauma of the explosion to my spine.

It was then that I heard one of my soldiers cry out in pain and then began to call out my name, "SGT Moore! SGT Moore!" He was in another bunker at the end of the row; I could not see him much at all due to the thick dust that the explosion had caused. Another NCO told me not to move and that he would look after my injured soldier. It tore me up inside knowing that one of my guys was hurt and calling for me and I was unable to help him.

There appeared to be a lull in the attack when a soldier from another unit helped me onto a flatbed truck full of other wounded. The enemy knew our SOPs all too well; they knew that when the attack slowed, the first responders would be trying to get the wounded to the closest aid station or hospital. While I was lying on that truck out in the open the alarm sounded again, "Incoming, Incoming!" I tried to get off the truck but could not move when a soldier grabbed me and pulled me down to the ground just as the rounds began to impact around us. He tried to cover me with part of his body while the ground shook. I was face down on the gravel parking lot as the concussion from the blast would literally raise me up off the ground while shoving gravel into my face. I was choking on the dust and smoke; to this day I have flashbacks when I smell sulfur.

CHAPTER TWENTY-TWO

PURPLE HEARTS AND WOUNDED SPIRITS

Throughout my tours I had been in several life-threatening events that I did not think I would live through, but nothing compared to this. Unable to move, I felt helpless. The force of the explosion alone coursing through my body was enough to make me lose consciousness. I saw my life pass before my eyes; it was my past and present laid out before me all at once. I could see my wife, my children, all of those who were dear to me and some who were not. I could see them all, each and every one of them all at the same time as if they could see me too. I reached out to them, almost touching when I was suddenly jerked backwards. I was being pulled away from those who loved me to face those that did not. It was then, in a moment of coherent thought, that I truly believed that the next explosion would be my last; I cried out to God for help.

I believe that the Lord calmed my spirit as I accepted my fate and I prayed for God to take me home to be with Him. Suddenly I felt like I had been raised up so I could look down upon my life, not to see all the evil that I had done but the wrongs that had been done to me. I heard the voice of God say that I was forgiven of my sins because of my faith in His son Jesus but that I had not forgiven others. I saw the Lord's hand reach into my chest and pull out a black heart. It was my heart turned dark from all the hurt done to me that I had never let go of, pain that festered into anger and fear.

I saw all of the evil acts that our Muslim enemies had done or caused others to do. I heard the voices of those who tormented and humiliated me all the way back through my childhood. Finally the darkest portion of my heart broke open and I saw the root of my pain, the cornerstone of my fortress of anger. That was the buried memory of being sexually abused as a young boy at the hands of an older man.

I was nine or ten years old and I can still see his face as he warned me not to say anything because my family would know what I had done and they would hate me for it. He even told me that it would be okay because he could tell that I "really needed this and when I got older I would appreciate his affection." I did not speak of this to anyone, even my wife, until I began to write this story.

The Lord used this near death event to cleanse my heart, spirit and mind of all of the darkness that I had held there for most of my life. I finally realized why I frequently felt crushed by the weight of that day when I was young. Looking back it was as if my life had stopped and I remained the injured child inside. It was why I felt afraid and angry at the same time throughout most of my life. It was why I became a police officer and a soldier. I would be the man that would protect others from that evil. I also believed that no one would ever hurt me again if I was the protector. I now had the means to stop them. I understood my gut level response to the Muslim violence toward my family and brother soldiers. The overwhelming sense of helplessness, a lack of control over events that had transpired when I was young had prepared me for my response toward the events following the 9/11 attack.

I was finally able to process what had happened throughout my life and was able to forgive everyone who I believed had hurt me. I was free at last; I felt like chains had been removed from around my neck, arms and legs. When He broke open each section of darkened heart He burned it up into a vapor with His light of truth and love. I expected to continue on into His presence at this point when I heard Him say, "Live with forgiveness." I asked to stay with Him in His light; I did not want to go back to such a dark world. Then, just as quickly as it had vanished, my life flashed before me again. I saw my friends, my children and finally my wife's sweet smiling face. She reached out to me and I was back.

I awoke to being back in the flatbed truck, racing across the base, while the Iraqi FO was calling in rounds at our truck. Mortars were landing around us and directly behind us but we were able to reach the hospital without further injury. I began to lose consciousness again but I remember being examined and treated by a medical team.

MY CO CPT PEARSON AND PLATOON LEADER 1LT MCCARROLL AFTER EACH RECEIVING THE BRONZE STAR; THIS IS WHAT GOOD LEADERSHIP LOOKS LIKE.

It was then that I saw my PL looking over me and reassuring me that I would be okay. I remember hearing the groans of other soldiers in the ER while the medical staff triaged all of the wounded. The next thing I remember was my PL helping to carry my stretcher out to the helicopter waiting to transport us to the main United States hospital in Baghdad near the embassy.

I was wheeled down the hall at the hospital to a horrific sight of wall-to-wall wounded soldiers. Along with striking our base, the enemy also fired upon the embassy, injuring scores of soldiers there. After I was stabilized, I was thrilled to see my brother-in-law Terry (Carole's husband) waiting for me. My PL knew of my relationship with Terry, and that he was currently stationed at the embassy, and contacted him about my status. Terry's presence had a calming effect on my heart; knowing that I was with a family member gave me a sense of peace. He was able to contact my family directly so my wife had heard from family even prior to the Army chaplain pulling up the driveway.

Over the next several months and years I had journeyed far both physically and spiritually. I was sent to an Air Force hospital initially for treatment and then eventually home to the VA hospital for recovery and therapy. I spent much of that time regaining my physical strength and well-being, and my emotional and spiritual as well-being. Much of the ongoing healing process was greatly aided by my wife and children and especially my brother Ray. He lived close by to us and was always a welcome sight and good company on a regular basis. I was finally able to put all of my wounds and injuries into perspective and release them. No longer was I carrying the pain that festered into anger, an unforgiving spirit, and fear. The Lord set me free!

In a span of another two years I was medically retired from active service having received the Purple Heart medal for my physical wounds and a healed spirit as well. It was during that time of rehabilitation that my VA therapist was helping me get a handle on my Post-traumatic stress. The combination of three combat tours had left me with a number of unsettled issues centered on regret and guilt, the burden carried by many combat soldiers. I initially resisted anything deeper than surface cooperation, just going through the motions. I had become very good at knowing what to share and what not to, I would not become vulnerable to anyone again.

One exercise that I agreed to participate in was a group session with other soldiers. I did not expect to be in a room with veterans from previous wars. One of the most powerful stories was shared by a World War II veteran. His experience during that conflict was so similar to mine in the realm of fear, guilt, regret and anger. Although that war was different on so many levels his experience as a combat soldier was painfully similar. The turning point for me was when he talked of how many decades he had kept his pain to himself which eventually led him to alcoholism and two failed marriages.

I was filled with fear and determination that I would not allow my family to suffer through my self-destruction. Nor did I want to be looking in the mirror decades from now with more regret than I currently carried. From that point forward I became my strongest advocate in search of an inner peace that would lead to a life worth living. I wanted to see the past in perspective, build upon it and move forward without becoming lost in a wilderness of darkness.

The next and most productive step was the counsel I received to write out my experiences on pen and paper. To physically see it and read it out loud, this helped me to minimize those demons that haunted me. The more I did that the less overwhelming the past became; I broke those chains one link at a time. This exercise is what has led me to write out my entire story. It was not just for me but to help my family to understand where I had been. It was also for other veterans as well. My prayer was that this might help veterans suffering from similar burdens. I hope they use my story as a place to begin their own journey of healing. I look forward to many more years of helping veterans heal their wounds and off load their burdens. The road before me will be difficult, yet worthy of all I have, God willing.

EPILOGUE

It has been over fourteen years since the 9/11 attack, over eleven years since my first tour overseas and seven years since my last. One of the most important discoveries of my journey is the realization that this is not just *my* journey. This story belongs to everyone, not just the veterans who deployed to combat zones but also the families they left behind. Those same families supported their deployed soldiers and kept their homes together. Those same families, friends and neighbors welcomed us home, not knowing how to help us transition, yet stepping up anyway.

My last tour ended in 2008 yet my family did not close down Mooremart. It started with me in 2004 but it had grown into so much more. The family and friends who make Mooremart work are dedicated to supporting any troops we have deployed for as long as they are deployed. To put their sacrifice into perspective, for the last six years they have been supporting the troops knowing that I would not deploy again, which is the heart of why they do what they do.

During my three tours I was obviously not the only soldier to return home dealing with PTSD, regret for having not done enough and guilt for what I had done. Some soldiers I knew returned home to self-destruct through addictions, failed marriages and eventually suicide. Yet others who experienced traumatic physical injuries and witnessed horrific acts of violence, returned to make each day count as best they could, regardless of the limitations they had both physically and emotionally. These soldiers are an inspiration to me as they should be to us all.

A great example of overcoming adversity is SGT Beck. He was a young soldier who was wounded during the same attack that I was and suffered the loss of both of his legs. Six years later I was honored to attend the ground-breaking ceremony for his new home. The organization Homes for our Troops along with other local businesses had come together to build a home for SGT Beck and his young family. To see this young man standing on prosthetic legs, holding his little girl in his arms with so many friends and family around him was moving and inspiring. SGT Beck is a good example of what we can overcome with the help of those who care enough to step up.

Soldiers who served with SGT Beck at the groundbreaking for his new home. (L to R) Brian Moore, Michael Beck, Melvin Kearney, and Ron Valenzuela.

During his farewell speech at West Point, General Douglas MacArthur uttered an eternal truth in regards to veterans, "Old soldiers never die, they just fade away." His words were timeless, poetic and yet painfully true. It seems that when a nation is at war all honor goes to the men and women who sacrifice so much for the defense of their country. It does not take long however for that honor to fade away when that grateful nation now views those veterans as a burden.

While flying home from Iraq for my father's funeral, still in my desert uniform, I overheard a passenger comment that he wished he could "kick my ass off the plane" so he would not have to be in my company. Fortunately the flight attendant responded quickly by suggesting, "Let's wait until we are at thirty thousand feet and we can kick your ass off the plane." He was silent for the remainder of the flight.

If history has taught us anything it is that human nature does not change. Veterans come in all forms, men and women, young and old with wounds of varying degrees. We do not look for trouble, but would rather it come to us than our children. Like the first patriots, we are men and women of ordinary courage who subjected themselves to unbelievable hardship and unspeakable horrors. We sought neither glory nor accolades, simply to return home in peace. The peace that comes from knowing we served honorably and that our families and friends will not face those same horrors.

I am home for good now but my journey continues. My journey through war, faith and forgiveness did not end my last day in Iraq; in fact it had barely begun. I would no longer carry my burdens alone for I finally saw that my God was with me all along. I have been asked by some "If you are a Christian then why did God let you to get injured?" My answer is that He allowed me to be injured so that he could save my life. It is my hope that those who read my story would begin their journey as well. Know that if you walk with God there is no place too evil or dark that His love cannot show you the way home.

Acronyms, Abbreviations, and Military Jargon

11B: Infantry MOS designation

1st SGT: "TOP" / E-8 / highest ranking NCO in a Company or Battery

ANA: Afghan National Army

ARNG: Army National Guard

ASAP: As Soon As Possible

A-top: Afghan Commander that was my counterpart

CAB: Combat Action Badge

CIB: Combat Infantry badge

Chinook: A large dual prop Army used to transport several men and their equipment.

CoC: Chain of Command

Coms: Communication

Crew Chief: The NCO in charge of the operation of a military aircraft other than flying.

CSM: Command Sergeant Major / E-9 / highest ranking NCO in a Battalion, Brigade or Division

C-wire: Constantina Wire, razor wire strung out like a horizontal slinky.

DeMOB: the process of mobilizing back from the war zone to eventual reunification with family.

DFAC: Dining facility

EOD: Explosive Ordnance Disposal

Flag Pole: Command HQ

FOB: Forward Operating Base

HQ: Head Quarters

ICT: Irrelevant Command Types

IED: Improvised Explosive Device

Intel: Intelligence

JFK: John F. Kennedy

K: Kilometer or Klick

Land Nav: Land Navigation

Latrine: Most versions of a military bathroom, from an actual building down to a hole in the ground.

LU: Line Units, A term used for standard Army groups of soldiers who worked under standard Army SOPs.

LW: Long Walks

LZ: Landing Zone, a "Hot LZ" is one under fire.

M.Ed.: Master's degree in Education

MOB: Mobilization

MOS: Military Occupational Specialty

MP: Military Police

MRE: Meals Ready to Eat

MSG: Master SGT / E-8

NCO: Non-Commissioned Officer

NG: National Guard

NH: New Hampshire

Outside the Wire: going outside of the FOB on a mission

Pak: Pakistan

PC: Politically Correct

PJ: Porta John

PL: Platoon Leader, usually a Lieutenant

Poop Soup: term for mixture of human waste and diesel fuel, stirred then burned

PP: Permanent Party

PR: Propaganda

PS: Platoon Sergeant

PTSD: Post-Traumatic Stress Disorder

PX/BX: Post Exchange/Base exchange

SF: Special Forces / Green Beret

SFC: Sergeant First Class / E-7 / Platoon SGT

SGT: Sergeant / E-5 / team leader

SL: Squad Leader

SOP: Standard Operating procedure

SSG: Staff Sergeant / E-6 / Squad Leader

Terps: Interpreters

TL: Team Leader

UK: United Kingdom

U.S.: United States

U.S.CG: United States Coast Guard

VA: Veterans Administration

VT: Vermont

YD: Yellow Dog

References

Bay, Michael. Dir. 2001. *Pearl Harbor*. Touchstone Pictures.

Gibson. Michael. Dir. 1995. *Braveheart*. Paramount Pictures.

Martin, James Kirby, ed. 2008 *Ordinary Courage: The revolutionary war adventures of Joseph Plumb Martin*. Malden, MA: Blackwell

Scott, R. Dir. 2001. *Black Hawk Down*. Sony Pictures.

Spielberg, Steven. Dir. 1998. *Saving Private Ryan*. Paramount Pictures.

Stone, Oliver. Dir. 1986. *Platoon*. Orion.

ABOUT THE AUTHOR

Since recuperating from his wounds incurred during his last tour, Brian Moore was medically retired from the United States Army. He and his wife currently run a small farm in central Virginia, while he is an inspirational speaker at churches, colleges and veteran organizations. He holds a master's degree in education.

CPSIA information can be obtained
at www.ICGtesting.com
Printed in the USA
FFOW02n1753230216

9 781935 986805